Railways & Recollections
Rails to the Yorkshire Coas

Phil Horton

Contents

Acknowledgements

British Library Cataloguing in Publication Data

A catalogue record for this book is available from the British Library.

Silver Link Publishing Ltd
The Trundle
Ringstead Road
Great Addington
Kettering
Northants NN14 4BW
Tel/Fax: 01536 330588

email: silverlinkpublishing@btconnect.com
Website: www.nostalgiacollection.com

Printed and bound in the Czech Republic

© Phil Horton 2017

First published in 2017

ISBN 978 1 85794 524 9

The idea for this book came from a conversation I had in the spring of 2017. My wife Sue and I had met up for lunch with an old colleague of mine, Dr John Mason, and his wife Ann, who now live in Somerset. Ann grew up in Hull and during lunch we got round to discussing my visit to a school friend there in 1964, together with my interest in Hull's various railway lines. In particular I recalled the host of level crossings in the city, and the work then going on to build new flyovers to replace two of them. Afterwards, reviewing the photos I had taken then, together with more recent ones I took while living near York in the 1980s, I realised that I had enough material for my second 'Recollections' book – of railways to the Yorkshire coast. I must therefore thank Ann for giving me the idea for the book, and to John for the use of his photo of a Duke of Burgundy butterfly.

While many of these 'Recollections' are my own, I have also obtained valuable information from *Modern Railways*, *Railway World* and *Railway Magazine*. Information on the closure dates of stations come from R.V.J. Butt's *The Directory of Railway Stations*, published by Patrick Stephens Ltd in 1995, while the building and scrapping dates for the various steam engines are from Hugh Longworth's *British Railway Steam Locomotives 1948-1968*, published by OPC in 2005.

I must also thank my wife Sue for her proofreading and editing of my text. Finally I would like to acknowledge the help and encouragement received from Peter Townsend of Silver Link Publishing Ltd and Will Adams of Keyword.

Phil Horton
Lincolnshire   September 2017

Title page: **SCARBOROUGH** Rails to the Yorkshire coast are certainly in evidence in this view looking towards Falsgrave signal box from the end of the very long Platform 1. The station and 120-lever signal box at Scarborough are Grade II listed. The fine gantry seen in the middle distance is no longer at Scarborough, having been donated to the North Yorkshire Moors Railway, where it can be found at Grosmont having been restored and put back into use. *Peter Townsend*

Introduction

My first book in Silver Link's 'Railways & Recollections' series, No 64: *The last years of BR steam around Bath*, describes how I first became interested in railways when I was growing up in that city in the 1960s. Here it was possible to see BR steam engines from all four of the pre-nationalised railway companies, although the

former London & North Eastern Railway (LNER) was represented by just a handful of Thompson-designed 'B1' 4-6-0s at Bath Green Park.

The present book describes my travels in Yorkshire in the early 1960s and again in the 1980s when I was living in the county. The area covered by these 'Recollections' includes the former East and North Ridings of Yorkshire, east of the East Coast Main Line between Doncaster and Northallerton, and from there northwards to Middlesbrough. Before nationalisation all was part of the LNER, while before the Grouping most of the lines were owned by the North Eastern Railway (NER). In the 1960s it was part of BR's North East Region BR(NER).

In the summer of 1960 my parents decided that we would tour North East England and Scotland in our Bedford Dormobile. The itinerary would include York and Scarborough. As a result, the number of ex-LNER engines underlined in my Ian Allan abc

Combined Volume increased significantly. Apart from a two-day shed-bashing trip to Yorkshire with the Bristol & District Railway Society in April 1963, the chance for a more extended visit occurred in the summer of 1964. By then I had acquired a second-hand Vespa motor scooter and was able to visit a school friend, whose family lived in Kingston-upon-Hull. We then went camping around Yorkshire before heading north as far as Edinburgh, visiting as many engine sheds as possible. These early trainspotting trips are described in Chapter 1.

Historically the area had boasted an extensive railway network, but by 1960 this had been significantly reduced by station and line closures. The process had started before the Second World War when, in 1931, the line from Gilling to Driffield lost its passenger service. Railway nationalisation saw the pace of closures increase and by the end of 1960 the stations at North and South Cave, Bubwith, Helmsley, Kirkbymoorside, Stokesley, Yarm and Staithes had all closed. Worse was to follow as the Beeching Report, published in March 1963, envisaged the closure of the stations at Whitby, Pickering, Pocklington, Market Weighton, Hornsea and Withernsea, together with many others. The lines concerned are shown on Map 1 and are listed in Appendix 1. At the same time steam power was being rapidly replaced by diesel multiple units (DMUs) and diesel-electric locomotives. By the time of my 1964 visit, Beeching's recommendations were being ruthlessly implemented. I had already travelled on many of the threatened lines in southern England and Wales and was therefore keen to include at least some of those in Yorkshire. My visits to these lines are described in Chapter 2 of this book.

Little did I know at the time, but some 20 years later in the summer of 1981 my work for the Nature Conservancy Council would bring me and my family to live near York. This was an ideal opportunity to become reacquainted with the railways of the

area. There was still plenty to see as the line from Middlesbrough to Whitby had survived the Beeching 'axe' and was being promoted as the 'Esk Valley Line'. In addition steam was once again operating on BR's main lines including the regular summer service from York, the 'Scarborough Spa Express'. Steam engines were also toiling up Newtondale again, operated by the heritage North Yorkshire Moors Railway (NYMR) between Pickering and Grosmont.

Things had also changed administratively. BR(NER) was now part of a larger Eastern Region, while the North and East Ridings of Yorkshire had been swept away by the Local Government Act of 1972. They had been replaced by the county of North Yorkshire and the deeply unpopular new county of Humberside. A small part of the North Riding had become part of the new county of Cleveland.

The second part of the book includes my 'Recollections' during this later period. Each of the remaining lines to the coast is described in turn, starting with those from Doncaster/Selby to Hull. The line along the coast between Scarborough and Hull is also included. The lines described are shown on Map 2. My photos also reflect a second dramatic change in the motive power scene: the replacement of both first-generation DMUs and diesel-electric locomotives on passenger trains by 'Pacer' and 'Sprinter' DMUs. A further brief visit to Yorkshire was made in 2017 and a number of photos, which compare and contrast the scene with that in the 1960s and 1980s, are also included.

While these 'Recollections' cannot hope to be comprehensive, I hope that they still give a flavour of the changing scene on the rails to the Yorkshire coast.

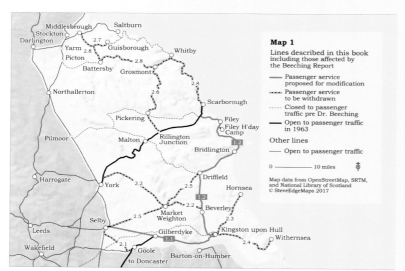

Map 1

Lines described in this book
including those affected by
the Beeching Report

— Passenger service
proposed for modification

— Passenger service
to be withdrawn

— Closed to passenger
traffic pre Dr. Beeching

— Open to passenger traffic
in 1963

Other lines

— Open to passenger traffic

0 ——— 10 miles

Map data from OpenStreetMap, SRTM,
and National Library of Scotland
© SteveEdgeMaps 2017

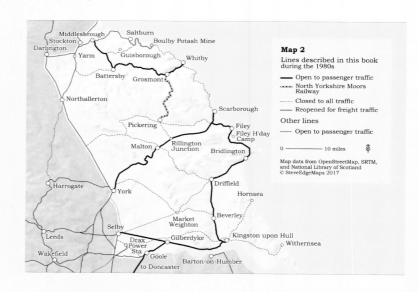

Map 2

Lines described in this book
during the 1980s

— Open to passenger traffic

···· North Yorkshire Moors
Railway

— Closed to all traffic

— Reopened for freight traffic

Other lines

— Open to passenger traffic

0 ——— 10 miles

Map data from OpenStreetMap, SRTM,
and National Library of Scotland
© SteveEdgeMaps 2017

My first ever visit to Yorkshire started at 6.45am on Friday 5 August 1960 when my parents and I left Bath for our annual camping holiday in our Bedford Dormobile. After an overnight stop near Crowle, we stopped briefly at Goole. While there a flagman appeared to stop road traffic and across the road came delightful ex-Lancashire & Yorkshire 0-4-0 saddle tank No 51222 hauling a train of wagons away from the town's extensive docklands. The engine was built at the L&Y's Horwich Works in 1901 and was withdrawn in March 1962. Later that year I was to discover that two of her classmates,

Nos 51217 and 51218, were shedded much closer to home at Bristol Barrow Road. No 51218 is now preserved on the Keighley & Worth Valley Railway and in March 2003 was taken to Goole Docks for a photo opportunity disguised as No 51222!

Our next stop was York and I was impatient to get in some trainspotting, but had to wait while we visited the Minster. Eventually we arrived at the station, which, on a summer Saturday, was very busy. While there I was able to take a few photos with my Box Brownie camera including ones of 'A4' 'Pacific' No 60006 *Sir Ralph Wedgwood* arriving with a train from the north, and 'V2' 2-6-2 No 60983

drifting light engine towards the station to take over an up express to King's Cross. A third photo is of another up express arriving behind English Electric Type 4 diesel-electric No D254 (later No 40054). This, together with the many DMUs present, was a portent for the future of steam.

After a short visit to Edinburgh we headed south again to Scarborough. While there I walked with my father back along the Seamer Road, which ran past the town's engine shed (50E). Among the engines there were two 'Hunt' 'D49' Class 4-4-0s, Nos 62739 *The Badsworth*, a Scarborough engine, and 62759 *The Craven*, from Starbeck shed, Harrogate

(50E). The class was designed by Sir Nigel Gresley for the LNER in 1927. Also present were several Class 'B16' 4-6-0s, originally designed by Sir Vincent Raven for the NER in 1920, although many were subsequently rebuilt by both Gresley and Edward Thompson for the LNER. A much more familiar engine was BR Standard Class 3 2-6-2 tank No 82026. These Swindon-built engines could be seen at both Bath Green Park and Bath Spa stations, and two of the class were at that time allocated to Scarborough shed and two to nearby Malton (50F). By 1960 their days in the North East were numbered as their duties had taken over by DMUs. After a short spell at York they were all transferred to BR(SR). One of the Malton engines, No 82029, then based at London's Nine Elms depot (70A), was one of the last two of the class to be withdrawn.

My next visit to Yorkshire was in April 1963 as one of a coach party organised by the Bristol & District Railway Society. Two of the engine sheds visited were York North (50A) and York South (by then a sub-shed of 50A). York North shed contained 71 steam engines together with a number of English Electric Type 4 diesel-electrics and diesel shunters. The most numerous class present were 18 Class 'V2' 2-6-2s, followed by 11 'B1' 4-6-0s, 'K2' 2-6-0s and 'WD' 2-8-0s. Other classes included a single 'B16/2', ex-LMS 'Black 5' and Standard Class 5 4-6-0s, and an ex-LMS 'Crab' 2-6-0. Express motive power was represented by six 'Pacifics': four 'A1s', one 'A3' and one 'A4', No 60019 *Bittern*. Two of the Standard engines, once shedded at Scarborough, were the previously mentioned 2-6-2T No 82029, and Standard Class 3 2-6-0 No 77004. During our visit one of the depot's ex-NER Class 'J27' 0-6-0s, No 65894, now preserved on the North Yorkshire Moors Railway, arrived with a load of coal for the depot's coaling plant.

At York South we found two more ex-Scarborough engines: Ivatt Class 2 and Standard Class

3 2-6-2s Nos 41251 and 82028. Two further 'J27s', Nos 65844 and 65888, both formerly of Malton shed, were also present. Other engines included four 'WDs', two 'V2s' and two 'A1s'. York South was shortly closed and its last roundhouse demolished.

 ## Summer 1964

A longer visit to Yorkshire occurred during the summer of 1964 when I visited my friend in Hull. I was looking forward to more shed-bashing in Yorkshire and the North East and had applied for permits for most of the sheds. The Public Relations and Publicity Officer at York replied that they did not issue individual permits, but instead included a list of dates when larger groups were to visit the sheds concerned, and we were issued with permits so that we could join them. I queried what would happen if the larger group did not turn up, only to be told that this was a very rare occurrence. In the event, although we tried to arrive at the depot on time, we did not once see any of the larger parties! Our permits were, however, honoured on every occasion and we visited a host of sheds in the North East of England including York and Hull (Dairycoates) (50B).

York shed, visited on 28 July, contained 72 steam engines. Again 'V2s' were the most numerous class, with 14 examples, while 'B1' 4-6-0s, 'K2' 2-6-0s and 'WD' 2-8-0s were all well represented. The number of 'A2' 'Pacifics' had increased from six (at both York sheds in 1963) to 11, while two of the three ex-NER 'J27' 0-6-0s were also recorded again, including the now preserved No 65894. There were several indicators of change in the local motive power situation since 1963, including the transfer

of the 2-6-2 tank engines to BR(SR). All six 'B16' 4-6-0s present had been withdrawn a month earlier and were stored awaiting their last journey to a scrapyard. A class not seen in 1963 were three of the seven BR Standard 9F 2-10-0s recently transferred to York from BR(WR) where they had been displaced by diesels. One of them, No 92006, was an old friend, as it had spent two months at Bath Green Park in the summer of 1961 working trains over the former Somerset & Dorset line to Bournemouth.

Two days later on 30 July I visited Hull (Dairycoates), which, since Botanic Gardens shed (50C) had become a diesel depot, was now the only steam shed in the city. It contained 26 steam engines of just three active classes: one 'V2' 2-6-2, seven 'B1' 4-6-0s and ten 'WD' 2-8-0s. In addition eight Class 'B16' 4-6-0s, all former York engines, were stored and destined for the breaker's yard. None of the class were preserved. I was to return to Dairycoates shed some 20 years later when it was the base of the Humberside Locomotive Preservation Group (HLPG), which had become the owner of ex-LMS 'Black 5' 4-6-0 No 45305 when it was donated to the group by Alderman Albert E. Draper; the locomotive would otherwise have been broken up at his scrapyard in Hull. The purpose of my visit, however, was to see the NRM's 'King Arthur' Class 4-6-0 *Sir Lamiel*, which the group was then restoring.

One distinctive memory of my stay in Hull was, in the middle of the night, hearing the clank of the 'WDs' as they made their way slowly around Hull to and from the Alexandra and Victoria Docks. As much of the land around Hull is flat, it was once a city of level crossings. The Hessle Road and Anlaby Road crossings were a particular source of frustration for motorists. At the time of my visit the Hessle Flyover had just been completed, while that on the Anlaby Road was under construction. Both sites offered vantage points to photograph any passing steam.

Left and below left: **YORK** The Scarborough platforms on the south-eastern side of York station gave good views of trains arriving from Scotland and the North of England up the East Coast Main Line (ECML). Here, on Saturday 6 August, during my first visit to Yorkshire, 'A4' 'Pacific' No 60006 *Sir Ralph Wedgwood* arrives with a train from the north followed a little later by English Electric Type 4 diesel-electric No D254 (later No 40054). No 60006, a King's Cross Top Shed (34A) engine, was built in 1938 and withdrawn in September 1965. No D254 had only been in service for a year, and was withdrawn in September 1978. The class's spell on top ECML duties was short-lived as they were soon replaced by English Electric's Type 5 'Deltic' diesel-electrics.

Opposite page top left: **YORK NORTH SHED 50A** On 22 April 1963 I was one of a coach party organised by the Bristol & District Railway Society to visit York North Depot (50A). During the visit ex-NER Class 'J27' 0-6-0 No 65894 arrived with a load of coal for the depot's imposing coaling plant. Built at Darlington in September 1923, the engine was not withdrawn from Sunderland shed (52G) until September 1967. Before it was transferred to Tyneside the 'J27' was specially turned out by York shed to work the last goods train from Kirkbymoorside to Malton. The engine was purchased from BR by the North East Locomotive Preservation Group (NELPG) and is now based on the North Yorkshire Moors Railway at Grosmont (see the photo on page 51).

Opposite page top right: **YORK NORTH SHED 50A** The Class 'B16' 4-6-0s were designed by Sir Vincent Raven, the CME of the North Eastern Railway. Seventy-nine of the three-cylinder engines were built at Darlington between 1919 and 1920 and for four decades hauled both goods and passenger trains in the North East; many were based at 50A. June 1964 saw a mass culling of the class and a month later, during a visit to York shed on 28 July 1964, I found six of them stored together with a number of 'V2s' and other ex-LNER engines. No 61448, pictured, was a 'B16/3', which had been rebuilt by Thompson in 1944 with individual sets of Walschaerts valve gear for each cylinder.

Left: **HULL (DAIRYCOATES) 50B**
I visited this depot on 30 July 1964 and found eight more 'B16s', stored and waiting for their final journey to the scrapyard; among them was No 61435, a Class 'B16/2'. The 'B16/2s' were Gresley rebuilds of 1937 with a Walschaerts valve gear on the middle cylinder only. Their final years were spent working holiday excursions to Scarborough, Bridlington and Filey. No 61435 still carries its last excursion reporting number, 1Z37.

Right: **HULL (DAIRYCOATES) 50B** Among the active engines at the depot on 30 July was a single Class 'V2' 2-6-2, No 60886 of Heaton shed (52B). Built in 1939, it was withdrawn in August 1966. Besides the 'B16s' the other engines at Dairycoates comprised seven Class 'B1' 4-6-0s and ten 'WD' 2-8-0s.

Below: **HULL** The level crossing on the Hessle Road out of Hull had caused delays for motorists for many years, but by 1964 this had recently been replaced by a flyover. Here one of the six Ivatt Class 4MT 2-6-0s allocated to Dairycoates shed, No 43069, approaches the new flyover with a train of imported timber on 27 July 1964. Although built to an LMS design, No 43069 was built at Doncaster in December 1950. It was withdrawn in September 1966.

Below right: **HULL** Class 'WD' 'Austerity' 2-8-0 No 90711 also approaches the new Hessle Flyover with a train of coal empties on the same day. Both goods trains have used the former Hull & Barnsley Railway line from Alexandra and Victoria Docks. The line to the right goes to Paragon station. One of Hull's recently acquired English Electric Type 3 diesel-electrics (later Class 37) has appeared, bottom left, heading for the station. No 90711 was built for the War Department at the Vulcan Foundry in February 1945, becoming BR No 90711 in December 1948. It was withdrawn in January 1967.

HULL The busy Anlaby Road level crossing in Hull was also once the bane of local motorists. In this view, taken on 30 July 1964, construction of the new flyover there was well under way as Class 'WD' 'Austerity' 2-8-0 No 90452 drifts past the signal box and over the crossing while running light engine to Dairycoates shed. The engine was also built at the Vulcan Foundry for the WD in April 1944, becoming BR No 90452 in January 1949. It was withdrawn in June 1965.

HULL A view in the opposite direction shows Class 'B1' 4-6-0 No 61010 *Wildebeest* of Dairycoates shed approaching the crossing with a short van train on the same day. The Darlington-built engine dates from November 1946 and was withdrawn 19 years later.

The Beeching years

One of my objectives in visiting Hull in 1964 was to travel on at least some of the lines in the North and East Ridings of Yorkshire threatened by closure in the Beeching Report. The Report included a comprehensive list of all loss-making passenger services and all loss-making stations on those lines that would remain open. In some cases services were listed for 'Modification', which usually meant that most if not all of the wayside stations would close. Within the area covered by this book seven services were to be withdrawn, while two were to be modified. A list of these lines is shown in Table 1 of the Report. Three of the seven services ran from Hull, to Hornsea and Withernsea on the coast, and the cross-county service to York via Beverley, Market Weighton and Pocklington. A further threatened service ran from Selby to Bridlington via Market Weighton and Driffield, although all its intermediate stations had closed back in September 1954. Maps 1 and 3 of the Report showed that each service carried at most between 5,000 and 10,000 passengers a year and that the passenger receipts at most of the wayside stations were less than £5,000 per annum. Both statistics were well below those considered necessary by Beeching to run a profitable passenger service operated by DMUs.

Sadly there was no time for me to travel on either of the lines that passed through Market Weighton, but I did succeed in travelling on the two branch lines from Hull (Paragon) to Withernsea and Hornsea. The promoters of both lines hoped to develop their towns as fashionable seaside resorts that would rival that being developed at Scarborough. Both termini were therefore built with excursion traffic in mind. The lines were opened by the Hull & Holderness and Hull & Hornsea railways on 27 June 1854 and 28 March 1864 respectively,

although they would soon became part of the NER.

My first visit, on Monday 27 July, was to Withernsea, 20¾ miles by rail from Hull. At the time there were 13 departures from Hull to Withernsea each weekday, although four of these had started running on 27 July and were withdrawn at the end of the summer service. Similarly, of the nine trains that ran on Sundays, five were withdrawn at the end of the summer.

Four days later I travelled to Hornsea Town, 15½ miles from Hull. Twelve trains then arrived at the town from Hull each weekday, three of which were withdrawn at the end of the summer. The Sunday service of eight trains was reduced to just four at the end of August.

DMUs had replaced steam on both branches early in 1957, and at the time of my visits the service was being worked by trains comprising two three-car Cravens units (later Class 105). The six-coach trains I used were all very well patronised, while both termini still included ample accommodation for excursion trains. A common criticism of the Beeching Report was that the survey of passenger numbers was carried out in April before the start of the holiday season. However, 1964 was to be the last summer that day-trippers would arrive at the two seaside towns by train, as both lines closed on 19 October. The trackbed of the Withernsea line is now a public footpath from the outskirts of Hull to the village of Keyingham. At Hornsea the trackbed forms part of National Cycle Route No 65, Hornsea to Middlesbrough, from Hornsea station to the centre of Hull.

My last two journeys on threatened lines in Yorkshire occurred a week later. These were from Malton to Whitby and from Whitby to Scarborough. Map 1 of the Beeching Report indicated that, between Rillington Junction and Grosmont, the

Whitby line carried a maximum of 5,000 passengers per week. Up to 10,000 were travelling between Grosmont and Whitby, but this line was also used by another threatened service, that between Middlesbrough and Whitby. The Beeching's Map 3 shows that only Malton, Pickering and Whitby Town stations had passenger receipts above £5,000. The takings at both Malton and Whitby were boosted by the York to Scarborough and Middlesbrough to Whitby trains respectively.

The 24-mile line from Whitby to Pickering was of considerable historic interest. It had been opened in 1836 by the Whitby & Pickering Railway (W&P) and was one of the first horse-drawn railways in Yorkshire, with George Stephenson as its engineer. A rope-worked incline was used to haul traffic up the northern escarpment of the North Yorkshire Moors from the Esk Valley at Grosmont to Goathland. Beyond Goathland the gradient became easier, taking the line up to the summit at Fen Bog, 550 feet above sea level. South of Fen Bog the line ran down to Pickering through Newtondale. In 1845 the W&P was absorbed by George Hudson's York & North Midland Railway (Y&NMR). The track was doubled and extended to join the York to Scarborough line at Rillington Junction. It became part of the NER nine years later. The rope-worked incline was later replaced by an adhesion-worked line, which ran via Beck Hole.

In the summer of 1964 six trains a day traversed the 35¼-mile line from Malton to Whitby (Town) each weekday, five of which had started at York. The 4.42pm Fridays-only train from Malton was of some interest as, during the summer, it included through coaches from King's Cross. This train last ran on 14 August 1964. On Saturdays the London train left Malton at 4.08pm, running until 29 August. At Grosmont the line from Malton joined the 35-mile

Esk Valley line from Middlesbrough to Whitby via Battersby Junction. Further details of this line, which survived the Beeching cuts, are given in Chapter 9.

Maps 1 and 3 of the Beeching Report showed that trains on the 23½-mile line along the coast from Whitby to Scarborough carried a maximum of 5,000 passengers per week, while of the seven intermediate stations only Robin Hood's Bay had annual passenger receipts above £5,000. The line had been a relative latecomer to the railway scene but, after a long struggle to raise finance, it finally opened in July 1885 as the Scarborough & Whitby Railway. It was operated by the NER from the start and soon became part of it. A station above Whitby (Whitby West Cliff) had already opened when the Whitby, Redcar & Middlesbrough Union Railway had finally completed its line from Middlesbrough in December 1883 (it closed in May 1958). To continue the line south to Scarborough involved the construction of the 915-foot-long, 125-foot-high Larpool Viaduct. Trains from Grosmont passed under this viaduct, while a steeply graded line was built up the north side of the Esk Valley from Whitby to join the Middlesbrough line at Prospect Hill Junction. These trains originally ran through to West Cliff station, but after this closed in June 1961 they reversed just beyond the junction's signal box. A further reversal was required outside Scarborough station from Londesborough Road signal box into Scarborough's Platform 1A.

In the summer of 1964 nine trains left Whitby for Scarborough each weekday, six of which had started at Middlesbrough and one at Darlington. A further train ran from West Hartlepool until 28 August. At the time of my visit trains were formed of two three-car Metropolitan-Cammell units (later Class 101). A single three-car Metropolitan-Cammell unit had earlier brought me up Newtondale from Malton to Whitby on 7 August 1964, while two more carried me to Scarborough and back. By

coincidence the last goods train from Whitby to Scarborough had run just two days earlier, worked by 0-6-0 DM shunter No D2151 (03151). Much to my surprise my train from Whitby back to Malton was hauled by one of York shed's 'B1' 4-6-0s, No 61319, which I had 'spotted' there earlier, with two packed non-corridor coaches. Given the improvised nature of the train, I assumed that it had replaced a failed DMU.

At Malton I left the train thinking that I would never travel by train up Newtondale or see a 'B1' at Whitby again. Despite vigorous lobbying from the local Conservative MP and the new Labour Government's pledge to review the Beeching Report, the services from Whitby to Malton and Scarborough were withdrawn on 6 March 1965. But as described in Chapter 8, the Pickering to Grosmont line opened again as the North Yorkshire Moors Railway in 1973.

In writing about the effects of the Beeching Report on rail services to the Yorkshire coast, mention must also be made of the dozens of extra trains that ran on summer Saturdays to Bridlington, Filey, Filey Holiday Camp and Scarborough. Dr Beeching had, however, calculated that, because the extra carriages were only used a few times a year, these services lost BR up to £3.5 million per year. Most of the old carriages were therefore soon scrapped and the trains withdrawn. By 1964 their number had already been reduced but, as shown in Appendix 2, a significant number still ran during that summer. Although a shadow of their former number, a handful continued to run into the 1990s.

Hull to Withernsea & Hornsea

HULL PARAGON Two Cravens three-car units (later Class 105) headed by No E50359 stand in Hull Paragon station forming the 1.15pm train to Withernsea on Monday 27 July 1964. This was one of four additional trains that commenced running to Withernsea that Monday at the start of the summer season. Although a locomotive-hauled set of coaches is visible to the right of the DMU, the platforms to its left are dominated by other units, including one built by Birmingham Railway Carriage & Wagon (later Class 104).

Above: **WITHERNSEA** The two Cravens three-car units headed by No E50359 have arrived at Withernsea as the 1.15pm service from Hull on that same July day. The train has arrived at the station's outer excursion platform. Passengers from the crowded train are being channelled by the perimeter fence to the exit in the main station buildings behind the photographer.

Above right: **WITHERNSEA** Passengers from the Hull train make their way out of Withernsea station through the main station buildings. Goods wagons can be seen in the goods yard to the left of the single platform. The service was listed for closure in the Beeching Report and the trains were withdrawn from 19 October 1964. The goods service followed in May 1965.

Right: **HORNSEA** The main platform at Hornsea (Town), well provided with seats, is shown together with the station buildings and overall roof. The two excursion platforms are visible to the left. Like the Withernsea branch, its passenger service was listed for closure in the Beeching Report. Both passenger and goods facilities were withdrawn on 19 October 1964.

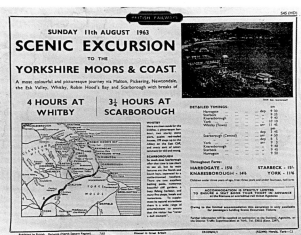

HORNSEA With one of the starter signals in the foreground, two Cravens three-car units (Class 105) pass the signal box at Hornsea (Town) forming the 5.25pm from Hull on 31 July 1964. On the right are the two signals for the excursion platform faces. The remains of the turntable pit can seen on the left. The DMUs will return to Hull at 6.05pm. Three additional trains ran from Hull to Hornsea for the summer, from 27 July.

Malton-Whitby-Scarborough and return

Above: **WHITBY** The three-car Metropolitan-Cammell DMU stands in Whitby station after arrival as the 1.50pm service from York on Tuesday 7 August 1964. Another DMU waits with a train in one of the two platforms on the right.

MALTON A three-car Metropolitan-Cammell DMU (later Class 101) arrives at Malton as the 1.50pm from York to Whitby on 7 August 1964. The unusual layout of the station can be seen, with its overall roof covering the single down line and with platform faces on each side. The up platform was to the left, outside the outer retaining wall of the overall roof. Instead of a footbridge, a moveable gangway gave access across the up platform; when the line was in use the gangway was run into a cavity below the platform. The former two-road engine shed is just visible in the background. The service was listed for closure in the Beeching Report and did so on 8 March 1965.

Right: **WHITBY** Two three-car Metropolitan-Cammell DMUs head for Scarborough via Larpool Viaduct above the Esk Valley outside Whitby on the same day. The train has climbed out of Whitby on the line to the right, which runs under Prospect Hill Junction signal box. Although the DMU appears to be running on double track, the second track forms part of a passing loop and only a single line ran over the viaduct.

Right: **WHITBY** The 3.41pm service from Whitby to Scarborough, which had left Middlesbrough at 2.15pm and has reversed at Battersby, now heads away from Prospect Hill Junction towards the viaduct and Scarborough. As with the service from Malton, Beeching's surveys showed that the service between Whitby and Scarborough was also carrying fewer than 5,000 passengers a week, and it also closed 8 March 1965.

Below: **WHITBY** I took this view of the Esk Valley as my train crossed Larpool Viaduct on that August day. The line climbing out of Whitby to Prospect Hill Junction is visible in the middle distance, while below it is the double track to Grosmont. The old gasworks sidings are visible in the bottom right, while Whitby Abbey can be seen on the horizon.

Below right: **WHITBY** Fifty-seven years later, on 14 August 2017, the view from Larpool Viaduct is very different. The north bank of the River Esk is now covered in trees and bushes. The allotments and former gasworks have disappeared, apart from a single brick building, while only the single railway track to Grosmont survives. Standard Class 4 2-6-0 No 76079 is seen approaching the viaduct with the NYMR's 14.00 service from Whitby to Pickering. The ruins of Whitby Abbey remain visible on the horizon as they have done for almost 500 years since Henry VIII dissolved the monasteries.

Right: **ROBIN HOOD'S BAY** Travelling in my DMU above the cliffs between Robin Hood's Bay and Ravenscar, I felt myself to be flying above the sea! Twenty-six years later, in August 1990, I returned to the area to walk the line, now a public foot/bridleway, from Whitby to Scarborough. Much of the Yorkshire coast line north of Flamborough Head displays a geological sequence similar to the more famous Jurassic Coast in Dorset. Because of this, much of it is notified as a Site of Special Scientific Interest (SSSI).

Below: **WHITBY** With the ruins of Whitby Abbey visible again in the background, Class 'B1' 4-6-0 No 61198 stands in the carriage sidings at Whitby with a return excursion on 7 August 1964. The engine was shedded at York (50A) and I had 'spotted' it there a week earlier. The photo was taken from the returning 5.32pm from Scarborough to Middlesbrough as it approached Whitby.

Right: **WHITBY** Another York-based Class 'B1', No 61319, also 'spotted' by me earlier, was the surprising choice for the 6.55pm all stations from Whitby to York on the same day. The train comprised just two non-corridor suburban coaches and was packed when it left Whitby, with many passengers standing. It was presumably a last-minute replacement for a failed DMU.

MALTON No 61319 has arrived safely at Malton with the 6.55pm service from Whitby to York. Malton signal box and the two avoiding lines are seen to the right of the engine. In my haste to photograph the train I have abandoned my crash helmet on the platform!

The 31-mile line from Selby to Hull was opened by the Selby & Hull Railway (S&H) in 1840. At Selby the line joined the Leeds & Selby Railway, which had arrived there in 1834. The H&S terminus at Hull Paragon opened in May 1848, by which time the line from Leeds was leased to the York & North Midland (Y&NM) and Manchester & Leeds (M&L) railways. The lease was taken over by the North Eastern Railway (NER) in 1854. Nine years later, in 1863, the Hull & Doncaster Railway, under the control of the NER, joined the S&H's line at Gilberdyke, 23¾ miles from Doncaster. In order to obtain Parliamentary consent for the line the NER had had to agree running rights over it for the Lancashire & Yorkshire Railway (L&Y) to Goole and Hull.

One hundred years later passenger services between Leeds, Selby and Hull were under the scrutiny of Dr Beeching. In his Report he proposed that the service should be 'Modified'. This would have involved the closure of four stations between Selby and Hull (see Appendix 1), but in the event Hemingborough was the only station to close, in November 1967.

In 1981 the chief passenger service from Doncaster to Hull via Goole was the hourly 'Trans Pennine Expresses', which ran from Manchester Piccadilly via Sheffield. These were still worked by Swindon-built Class 123 'Trans Pennine' units, which had been introduced in January 1961. The service then ran between Hull and Liverpool Lime Street via Manchester Exchange and Leeds. In May 1979 these services were diverted to run via Doncaster and Sheffield, but by then the units were feeling their age. The original six-car formations had lost their buffet cars and were now running as four-car sets. The units were joined at Hull by similar Class 123 units, Swindon-built in 1963, which had been made redundant by BR(WR). The Liverpool trains ran

instead to Newcastle via York and were loco-hauled with a connection for Hull at Leeds. Local services from Doncaster to Hull were worked by either a DMU or Class 31 diesel-electric. One 'Deltic'-worked train left Hull for London King's Cross at 07.10 as the 'Hull Executive' (Saturdays excepted); it arrived back at Hull at 19.56. The Selby line, which joined that from Doncaster at Gilberdyke, saw the hourly Class 31-worked connecting services off the Liverpool to Newcastle trains together with a number of DMU-worked locals. Several of the intermediate stations, including South Milford, Howden and Eastrington, saw a very poor service, especially on weekdays.

It was the service between Doncaster and Hull, however, that came under threat in 1984. The swingbridge over the River Ouse north of Goole required major work and, for a time, it looked as if Goole would become the terminus of a branch line from Doncaster. However, after a generous donation from Humberside Country Council, reported to be £800,000, BR agreed to carry out the work and the line remains open today. 1984 also saw the 150th anniversary of the Leeds to Selby line. This was celebrated by a special train on 22 September headed by 'A4' 'Pacific' *Sir Nigel Gresley*, which ran from Leeds to Selby, then continued through Brough to Scarborough via Bridlington. After the Selby diversion of the East Coast Main Line opened in 1983, Selby lost its through ECML trains to London.

By the end of the decade the 'Trans Pennine' units and 'Deltics' had long gone, while the other diesel-electric classes and first-generation DMUs were being rapidly replaced by 'Pacers' and 'Sprinters'. By 1990 the route of the Hull to Manchester 'Trans Pennine' service had changed again, with trains running from Manchester Piccadilly to Hull via Leeds and Selby once more. Most of the Doncaster to Hull trains started at Sheffield.

The daily 07.00 departure from Hull was a through train to King's Cross via Goole. Local trains through Selby ran between York and Hull, Leeds and Hull and between York and Doncaster; the latter reversed at Selby. Another change to train services during the period was the reduction in the number of extra trains run on summer Saturdays from the industrial cities of the North to Bridlington via Gilberdyke (see Appendix 1). These had declined to just one, to Leicester.

By 2017 the passenger services over the lines had improved enormously. Selby saw services to King's Cross restored when, in September 2000, Hull Trains was granted an Open Access Licence to run trains between Hull and London via Selby. These are now operated by the First Group, which runs seven trains from Hull each weekday. Virgin Trains also ran a competing service to King's Cross, which leaves Hull at 07.00 (06.50 on Saturdays), calling at Selby and Doncaster. In addition Selby also sees TransPennine Express and Northern services between Hull and Manchester Piccadilly and between Hull and York respectively. Services from Doncaster to Hull were operated by Northern, which ran an hourly service from Sheffield with several trains continuing to Bridlington.

Although the photographs in this chapter concentrate on the passenger services, there is a glimpse of the remaining freight facilities at Goole Docks in the 1980s. Limited rail-freight facilities were still available at both Hull and Goole Docks in 2017. Traffic in 2017 included steel between both docks and the Rotherham Steel Terminal carried by DB Cargo. Hull Docks also handled trains of gypsum. Other freight at Goole included regular deliveries of sand to Goole Glassworks from Middleton Towers near Kings Lynn, carried by GB Railfreight.

Right: **DONCASTER** The Class 124 'Trans Pennine' DMUs were built as six-car sets at Swindon Works from 1960. By the 1980s they had been reduced to just four cars, but were still working trans-Pennine services between Hull and Manchester Piccadilly. One of the units arrives at Doncaster with a Hull to Manchester Piccadilly service during the spring of 1982. All the Class 124 units had been withdrawn by the end of 1984.

Below: **DONCASTER** BR Class 31/4 AIA-AIA diesel-electric No 31425 (No D5804/31274) approaches Doncaster with the 07.43 service from Hull to Cardiff Central on 6 May 1986. This was the only through train of the day between Hull and Cardiff. The next arrival at Doncaster from Hull was the '125'-worked 08.00 from Hull to King's Cross. No 31425 was withdrawn in December 1991.

Right: **GOOLE** By the 1980s rail traffic from Goole Docks was a shadow of that in 1960, when I encountered ex-L&Y Class 0-4-0ST No 51222 crossing a road in the town. Two Class 08 diesel shunters were, however, still required to handle the traffic. Nos 08168 (D3236) and 08567 (D3734), both allocated to Hull (Botanic Gardens), are seen in the dock sidings at Goole from the A161 Normandy Way overbridge on 19 April 1986, with a forest of crane jibs still present in the background. After withdrawal in March 1988, No 08168 had a spell in preservation at the Battlefield and Bluebell heritage railways. It is now reported to be in use at Nemesis Rail's Burton-upon-Trent base. No 08567, now owned by Arlington Fleet Services, is in use at their Eastleigh depot.

Right: **GOOLE** The view looking east from the A161 overbridge at Goole on 11 August 2017 has changed markedly since 1986. The railway lines remaining appear to run through birch woodland, although the town's two water towers, the 'Salt & Pepper Pots', confirm the photo's location. The view to the west in 1986 *(see overleaf)* has changed even more, with only a single head-shunt visible among the trees. Despite appearances the port still has a dedicated rail-freight terminal.

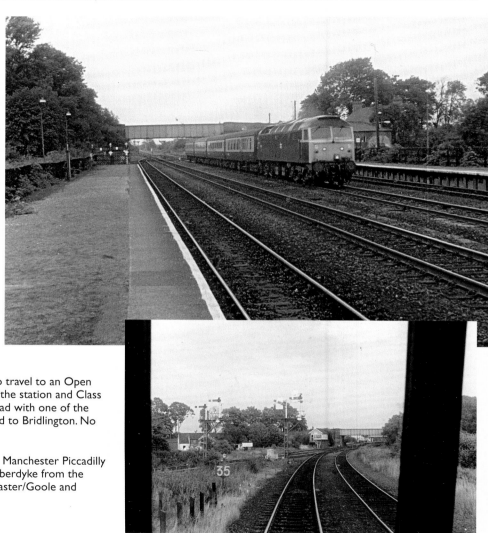

Above: **GOOLE** Looking west from the flyover, a further
expanse of sidings is visible. Here English Electric Type 3 Class 37
Co-Co diesel-electric No 37130 (D6830) awaits its next call of
duty. The engine was withdrawn in August 1992 following damage
in a collision at Skipton.

Above right: **GILBERDYKE** The lines from Doncaster and
from Leeds to Hull met at Gilberdyke, east of Goole. On
Saturday 28 July 1984 myself, my son and a friend used the station to travel to an Open
Day at Doncaster Works. Four tracks were then still in use through the station and Class
47 diesel-electric No 47522 (D1105) passed on the down centre road with one of the
few remaining summer-Saturdays-only trains, the 08.44 from Sheffield to Bridlington. No
47522 was withdrawn in December 1998.

Right: **GILBERDYKE** Returning from the Open Day on the 13.41 Manchester Piccadilly
to Hull train, I took this view of the junction for the Selby line at Gilberdyke from the
front seat of the DMU. The station saw arrivals from both the Doncaster/Goole and
Leeds/Selby lines at approximately 2-hourly intervals.

Below: **SELBY** Until October 1983 Selby was an important intermediate station on the East Coast Main Line. ECML trains were then diverted away from the town to avoid possible subsidence from the new Selby coalfield. The coal mines were, however, found to be uneconomic and were closed a few years later. In this view looking south the two through lines, once used by expresses to and from King's Cross, are still in place but are clearly out of use by May 1986.

Above: **GILBERDYKE** The four tracks through Gilberdyke station have now been reduced to two in this view from 11 August 2017, although the line is still controlled by semaphore signals from the signal box just beyond the overbridge. Two individual starter signals still control access to the Doncaster and Selby lines as in 1984. Here 'Pacer' unit No 142016 is signalled for Doncaster as it leaves the station forming the 12.19 Northern service from Hull to Doncaster. In the distance a Class 158 'Sprinter' can be seen approaching as Northern's 11.41 service from Sheffield and Doncaster to Hull. Although the two platforms have been reduced in length, they have been widened across the space previously occupied by the up and down slow lines.

Right: **SELBY** Looking north, a two-car Class 101 DMU waits in the bay platform at Selby forming the 07.38 service from York to Doncaster in May 1986. Trains from Selby to London were restored in September 2000 when Hull Trains commenced running between Hull and King's Cross via the town. Today the station also sees TransPennine Express services between Manchester Piccadilly and Hull, together with Northern trains between York and Hull.

Below left: **NORTH HOWDEN** Travelling south on the B1228 from Sutton-on-Derwent to join the M18 at Howden involves using the level crossing adjacent to Howden station. The station became North Howden in July 1922 to distinguish it from the town's Hull & Barnsley (H&B) station, which became South Howden. It became Howden again in June 1961. The station's rather unusual layout, with both station buildings and up platform west of the level crossing, is seen in this view on Saturday 19 April 1986. The down platform is to the east of the crossing.

Far right: **NORTH HOWDEN** A two-car Class 101 DMU is viewed from the level crossing as it pauses at the down platform at Howden as the 13.20 service from Leeds to Hull on 19 April 1986. The service between Leeds and Hull via Selby was listed for 'Modification' in the Beeching Report and four stations were listed for closure. In 1986 the service from Howden was poor: the arrival of this train at 14.02 was the first eastbound service since 07.58.

NORTH HOWDEN Thirty-one years later, on 11 August 2017, the former station buildings at Howden, now in private ownership, remain much as they did in 1987. The signal box is now closed and boarded up, while the semaphore signals have disappeared. The train service is immeasurably better, with seven through trains each weekday between Hull and London King's Cross operated by Hull Trains, together with an hourly Northern service between Hull and York. Here Hull Trains' Class 180 'Adelante' DMU No 180130 has arrived at Howden forming the 11.48 service from King's Cross to Hull.

Left: **SOUTH HOWDEN** In the early 1980s the remains of the old Hull & Barnsley Railway's South Howden station were still largely intact and could be viewed from the bridge that carried the B1228 over the long-closed line. The station had closed to passengers on 1 August 1955 although it was used occasionally for excursion traffic. Goods traffic ceased from 6 April 1959. When pictured on 19 April 1984 the once substantial station buildings are about to be demolished to make way for a housing estate. The overbridge was dismantled at the same time.

The 42-mile line from York to Scarborough was opened by the York & North Midland Railway (Y&NMR) in July 1845 but soon became part of the NER. The most important intermediate station was at Malton, situated on the River Derwent, 21 miles from York. Several branch-line junctions once existed east of Malton, including those to Gilling, Driffield and, at Rillington, to Pickering and Whitby. In addition, at Seamer, 3 miles from Scarborough, lines from both Pickering via Wykeham (see Appendix 1) and from Bridlington and Hull joined the Scarborough line. Of these only the line to Bridlington remains (see Chapter 6).

Scarborough was soon the largest spa and holiday resort on the North East coast. The NER had opened an excursion platform, some half a mile west of Scarborough station, in 1908. This became known as Scarborough Londesborough Road under the LNER in June 1933, while the main station became Scarborough Central. By this time the heavy tourist traffic had forced the LNER to close all but two of its wayside stations between York and Scarborough; 13 were closed in 1930, with only Malton and Seamer remaining. The flood of holiday trains was clearly more profitable than the meagre takings from the wayside stations. The holiday trains running in the summer of 1964 are shown in Appendix 2. By the end of the 1950s the number of holiday trains began to decline and Londesborough Road was closed by BR in August 1963.

In 1981 the ordinary weekday service was poor at approximately hourly, the trains starting at either Huddersfield, Leeds or York. One train, which arrived at 20.12, came from Manchester Victoria. Summer Saturdays at Scarborough in the summer of 1981 were still busy, with some 13 extra trains arriving at the resort. These included trains from Manchester Victoria, Birmingham New Street, Glasgow Queen Street and Newcastle. The 09.48 and 10.55 arrivals from Huddersfield and 10.55 from Hebden Bridge respectively reversed at Scarborough to reach Filey and Bridlington. Many of these trains were loco-hauled, which required a station pilot to be kept at Scarborough, at that time a Class 03 diesel shunter.

By the middle of the decade a new loco-hauled trans-Pennine service was introduced between Scarborough and Liverpool Lime Street via Manchester Victoria, Leeds and York. The trains ran every 2 hours on weekdays, arriving at Scarborough between 10.28 and 17.29. Initially they were hauled by Class 45 diesel-electrics, but these were later replaced by Class 47s. Apart from a late-morning arrival from Bradford Exchange, all other trains originated at York. Local trains were worked by first-generation DMUs. Two further trains ran during the week in summer from Sheffield and Wakefield Westgate. These trains started from Chesterfield and Manchester Victoria respectively on Saturdays and ran through to Bridlington. Seven other long-distance trains still arrived on Saturdays including ones from Leicester, Glasgow Queen Street and Newcastle, the latter continuing to Filey. A station pilot was still needed at Scarborough, but after 1984 a Class 08 was used.

Shortly before the Class 45s were replaced I remember seeing one of the class in trouble. I was attending a site meeting in a field adjacent to Seamer station where gravel working was proposed. During our meeting I noticed Scarborough's 08 shunter trundling along the line towards York. My curiosity was satisfied when some time later it reappeared hauling a Class 45 together with its train from Liverpool. How long, I wondered, had the passengers been waiting for rescue? Today, in the generally loco-free world of Britain's passenger trains, the wait I'm sure would be much longer! Today the field in question is a nature reserve.

In 1990 the introduction of Class 156 'Sprinter' DMUs had seen a greatly improved service between Scarborough and Manchester Piccadilly. Trains then ran hourly between 09.15 and 23.12, while two 'Pacer'-worked services started from Leeds, with one train from Sheffield. On summer Saturdays additional long-distance trains arrived from Leicester, Glasgow Central and Liverpool Lime Street.

Today an hourly service is provided between Liverpool Lime Street and Scarborough by TransPennine Express using three-car Class 185 'Desiro' DMUs.

Above left: **YORK** English Electric Type 4 Class 40 diesel-electric No 40103 (D303) leaves York with what is thought to be the 08.33 service from Wakefield Westgate to Scarborough on Wednesday 29 July 1981. The class, first introduced in 1958, were nearing the end of their active careers on BR, and No 40103 was withdrawn in February 1982.

Above right: **YORK** Some six years later, on 28 February 1987, the 'Sprinter' takeover at York is almost complete. On the left, standing in the Scarborough bay platforms, are Class 150 'Sprinters' Nos 150222 and 150224 in BR Regional Railways livery. Behind them 'Pacer' No 144003 can be seen in West Yorkshire Metro livery. On the right is one of the surviving first-generation Metropolitan-Vickers Class 101 DMUs, comprising Nos E53196 and E53244.

Left: **KIRKHAM ABBEY** Kirkham station was opened by the York & North Midland Railway (Y&NMR) in July 1845. It was renamed Kirkham Abbey in June 1875 by the NER in the hope of attracting tourists to the ruins of the nearby Priory. Although the station closed in September 1930, the attractive Y&NMR signal box remained together with the level crossing at the foot of Blue Hill. Here a road descends the north side of the Kirkham Abbey Gorge to cross the River Derwent south of the railway. Kirkham Abbey signal box is pictured on 12 August 1989. The box is now a listed building and, in August 2017, still controlled the signals protecting the level crossing.

Right: **KIRKHAM ABBEY** Over the years Scarborough has not fared well as far as through trains to London are concerned, apart from on summer Saturdays. During the summer of 1989 a single train, the 13.49 from Scarborough, ran to King's Cross via Leeds between 20 May and 2 September. A Class 125 HST is seen approaching the signal protecting Kirkham Abbey level crossing forming that service on 12 August 1989. In earlier years a 'Deltic' Class 55 diesel-electric might have been involved.

Below: **KIRKHAM ABBEY GORGE** With the River Derwent in the foreground Brush Type 4 diesel-electric Class 47/4 No 47426 (D1534), with the 'large logo' livery, leaves the Kirkham Abbey Gorge with the 09.05 Liverpool Lime Street to Scarborough train on 5 May 1985. These duties were soon to be taken over by Class 156 'Sprinter' DMUs. No 47426 was withdrawn in December 1992.

Below right: **KIRKHAM ABBEY GORGE** A three-car Class 101 DMU heads for York from Scarborough beside the River Derwent at the eastern end of the Kirkham Abbey Gorge, on a rather misty morning on 5 May 1985. These first-generation DMUs were also soon to be replaced by 'Sprinter' and 'Pacer' units.

Above: **HUTTONS AMBO** In this view a BR/Sulzer Class 45 diesel-electric is crossing the River Derwent at Huttons Ambo during September 1983 with the 16.00 train from Scarborough to Liverpool Lime Street. These engines were soon to be replaced by Class 47s before their duties were in turn taken over by 'Sprinter' DMUs.

Above right: **MALTON** Class 156 'Sprinter' No 156475 has arrived at Malton as the 15.33 Scarborough to Manchester Piccadilly service on 1 September 1990, after the 'Sprinter' takeover of the service. The outer island platform has been demolished and all trains now call at the former down platform. A single through line, which bypasses the station, is still in situ to the left, together with a goods loop.

Right: **MALTON** Not too much has changed in this view of Malton taken on Sunday 13 August 2017. The Class 156 'Sprinters' have been replaced by Class 185 'Desiro' DMUs operated by TransPennine Express. One of the units is seen calling at Malton forming the 10.21 service from Liverpool Lime Street. Although all semaphore signals have been replaced by colour lights, the level crossing at the east end of the station is still controlled from the adjacent signal box.

Right: **SEAMER** The scene around Seamer station has been transformed by the building of the A64 relief road, visible to the left of the photograph. The work included replacing the level crossing east of the station with a bridge for the B1261, from which this photo was taken on 14 August 2017. A TransPennine Express Class 185 'Desiro' DMU pauses at the much simplified station. Since the 120-lever signal box at Londesborough Road, Scarborough, closed in October 2010, all train movements in the area have been controlled from the former Seamer East signal box, seen here.

Above: **RILLINGTON JUNCTION** Like other wayside stations on the York to Scarborough line, that at Rillington, the junction for Pickering and Whitby, closed in September 1930. The passenger service from Whitby to Malton was withdrawn on 8 March 1965 although the junction remained for another year for goods traffic to Pickering. The signal box remained in use to work the level crossing and was pictured on 7 October 1990.

Right: **SEAMER** This is the view from the island platform at Seamer on Tuesday 21 August 1984. A semaphore signal, controlled by Seamer East signal box, protects the level crossing. The main station buildings are on the left. Today the open fields in the background are crossed by the A64 relief road. The level crossing has now been replaced by an overbridge.

Above: **SCARBOROUGH** In 1980 many of the trains to and from Scarborough were still loco-worked and a station pilot was required to shunt stock. Following the end of steam, these duties were performed by Class 03 BR 0-6-0 diesel-mechanical shunters. Here No 03089 (D2089), complete with its shunter's truck, hauls a rake of coaches out of the station on 29 July 1981. The engine was among the last of its class at Scarborough but was later used on similar duties at Norwich Thorpe until withdrawal on 6 November 1987. It is now preserved at the Mangapps Farm Railway Museum in Essex.

Above right: **SCARBOROUGH** By 1987 station pilot duties at Scarborough were in the hands of BR/English Electric 0-6-0 diesel-mechanical shunters. Performing these duties on 26 April 1987 is No 08525 (D3687). In 1985 the York-based engine had been officially named *Percy the Pilot!* It was still active at Neville Hill Depot, Leeds, in 2016. The rake of chocolate and cream Mark 1 coaches in the long excursion platform in the background will form the return 'Scarborough Spa Express' to York hauled by 'A4' 'Pacific' No 4468 *Mallard*. The set had been created by BR(WR) for the ill-fated 'GWR 150' celebrations the previous year.

Left: **SCARBOROUGH** Three- and two-car 'Pacers' Nos 144020 and 142024 leave Scarborough forming the 14.58 service for Leeds on Saturday 1 September 1990. The 'Pacers' are in West Yorkshire Metro and Regional Railways liveries respectively. The long excursion platform with its 'longest station seat' is on the left, although the fine gantry of semaphore signals, seen on page 36, has been replaced by colour light signals.

SCARBOROUGH

Class 156 'Sprinter' No 156475 in BR's Regional Railways livery approaches Scarborough past Londesborough Road signal box forming the 12.51 service from Manchester Piccadilly on 1 September 1990. The signal box is still operating an array of semaphore signals, which controlled movements in and out of the station. The box closed and the semaphore signals were replaced in October 2010. On the left is the entrance to the now disused Falsgrave Tunnel, through which I arrived at Scarborough from Whitby in July 1964. Additional carriage sidings for excursion stock were also accessed through this tunnel.

When BR relaxed its ban on steam in 1971, steam specials started to reach Scarborough. Their engines were turned on the triangle of lines that gave access to Filey Holiday Camp station, but when that station closed in September 1977 this was no longer an option. Fortuitously in 1980 Scarborough Borough Council was planning to relaunch the coastal town as a major spa, and was quick to recognise the benefits that the influx of visitors from steam specials would bring to the town. After negotiations with BR the Council agreed to make a substantial contribution to reinstating the turntable at Scarborough, the pit of which was still intact together with its water tank. A redundant 60-foot turntable at Gateshead was recovered and moved to Scarborough. The train, the 'Scarborough Spa Express' ('SSE'), was funded by BR and was shown in BR's 1981 timetable under 'Steam excursions operated by British Rail'. The engines used came from the pool of the Steam Locomotive Operators Association (SLOA).

The first 'SSE' was a VIP special on 25 May, the Spring Bank Holiday Monday, behind ex-LMS 'Coronation' 'Pacific' No 46229 *Duchess of Hamilton*. On arrival at Scarborough it was welcomed by the Lady Mayoress with a reception at the Grand Spa Hotel, which reopened on the same day. The public 'SSEs' ran on Tuesdays between 14 July and 25 August and Wednesdays between 29 July and 26 August, with a further run on August Bank Holiday, 31 August. Each day the train made two runs to Scarborough and back, leaving York at 09.50 and 16.35. The fare was just £4.75 for adults, £2.50 for children, but advance booking was required. Due

to problems with the 'Duchess', ex-LNER 'A3' 'Pacific' No 4472 (BR No 60103) *Flying Scotsman* was brought in as a substitute for the first public trains.

BR considered that the 1981 season had been a financial success but made a number of changes for the 1982 season. The train now left York at 08.45 and ran to Leeds via Harrogate before returning to York and Scarborough. After arrival back at York it followed the same route in reverse. Pre-booking was not required, and instead normal fares were changed with a £1.00 steam supplement for adults, a sum that was to increase slowly over the years. BR pointed out that this involved 212 miles of steam running for just £7.30! In addition railcard discounts also applied. The trains ran on Tuesdays and Wednesdays from 13 July and on Sundays from 1 August. The last train was on August Bank Holiday. The new format suited me personally as, with my young son and Family Railcard, I was able to catch the returning train at York and travel to Leeds, Harrogate and back to York. The climb at 1 in 100 from Leeds to Bramhope Tunnel south of Harrogate required some hard working by the engine. Making their debuts on the train in 1982 were ex-SR Bulleid 'Pacific' No 34092 *City of Wells*, ex-LMS 'Black 5' 4-6-0 No 5305 (BR No 45305), and ex-SR 4-6-0s Nos 777 (BR No 30777) *Sir Lamiel* and 850 *Lord Nelson* (BR No 30850).

A similar pattern was followed for the 1983 and 1984 seasons, although in 1984 trains ran on Thursdays rather than Wednesdays. The first public 'SSE' in 1983 ran on Tuesday 12 July behind *Sir Lamiel* while the NRM's 9F 2-10-0 No 92220 *Evening Star* made its appearance later in the season. The highlight was the arrival in August of privately owned 'A4'

'Pacific' No 60009 *Union of South Africa*.

In 1985 the 'SSE' season began on Tuesday 23 July, but in order to eliminate the stop of 20 minutes for water in York station BR decided that two engines should work the train, one from York to Leeds and back to York and another from York to Scarborough. In retrospect I wonder whether the expense of providing a second engine really outweighed the operational advantages. The season was dominated by just two engines, *City of Wells* and *Sir Lamiel*, assisted occasionally by *Evening Star*. Although the NRM's ex-LNER Class 'V2' 2-6-2 No 4771 (BR No 60801) *Green Arrow* worked the train on Sunday 25 August, it later failed and did not reappear that year. 1985 seemed to mark a decline in the fortunes of the 'SSE', possibly because of the lack of variety in its motive power. BR reported that the trains had an average loading of only 60% and that their future was under review.

In February 1986 BR announced that the train had been cancelled. The reasons given were that the prestigious engines, required to attract the punters, were needed elsewhere and that the rake of Mark 1 coaches was life-expired. However, *Mallard*'s restoration, much of it paid for by Scarborough Borough Council, was now complete. As the Borough had received an undertaking from BR that the engine would visit Scarborough at least once a year, BR was forced to run the 'SSE' on six Sundays in July and August, together with August Bank Holiday. The train made two return runs between York and Scarborough as in 1981, using the rake of Mark 1 coaches that BR(WR) had painted in chocolate and cream to work steam specials during its GWR 150th anniversary celebrations. The first and last 'SSEs' of 1986 were worked by *Mallard*. *Green Arrow* was also now available, while in August the NRM's ex-GWR 4-4-0 No 3440 *City of Truro* also appeared on the train. When these three engines were not available the train's loading was disappointing.

A limited number of 'SSEs' ran in both 1987 and 1988. 3 July 1988 saw the 50th anniversary of *Mallard*'s record-breaking 126mph run. A special train was organised by the NRM using the set of Mark I coaches from Bounds Green. This started from King's Cross hauled by BR's Class 98 prototype electric No 89001 (later named *Avocet*), making its first public appearance. *Mallard* took over the train at Doncaster for the run to Scarborough, stopping at York for lunch. Nevertheless, declining receipts, and disputes between the locomotive owners and BR over the fees paid for their use, led to the demise of the 'SSE'. Electrification work at York and Leeds was also considered by BR to be incompatible with the use of steam engines. The last of BR's 'SSEs' ran on Sunday 4 September 1988, hauled by *City of Truro*.

Since then Scarborough has seen occasional steam- and diesel-hauled specials promoted by a number of organisers. More recently the concept of the 'SSE' has been resurrected by West Coast Railways, whose trains have started, diesel-hauled, from the company's depot at Carnforth, and have then run to York via either Hellifield and Leeds or via Lancaster and Wakefield, where one of WCR's steam engines takes the train to Scarborough and back.

The 'Scarborough Spa Express', 1981

Below: **YORK** The first 'Scarborough Spa Express' carrying VIPs to Scarborough ran on 25 May 1981, Spring Bank Holiday Monday, hauled by ex-LMS 'Coronation' 'Pacific' No 46229 *Duchess of Hamilton*. The 'Duchess' then required attention and was replaced by ex-LNER 'A3' 'Pacific' No 4472 (BR No 60103) *Flying Scotsman* for its first public runs. Here 'Scotsman' backs down into York station, prior to working the first of two 'SSEs', due to depart at 09.50, on Wednesday 29 July 1981.

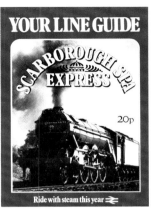

Above: A leaflet produced for the first year of the 'Scarborough Spa Express' in 1981.

Below left: **STRENSALL COMMON** 'A3' 'Pacific' No 4472 *Flying Scotsman* returns from Scarborough with the 'SSE' on 29 July 1981. 'Scotsman' was due to return to Scarborough for the second time at 16.35. The train is seen passing Strensall Common, a nationally important heathland Site of Special Scientific Interest (SSSI), for which I was responsible while working at York.

The 'Scarborough Spa Express', 1982

Right: **MALTON** 1982 saw the 'Scarborough Spa Express' extended to include the York-Harrogate-Leeds-York circuit in the morning. The return train, which left Scarborough at 17.20, traversed the circuit again but in reverse. Ex-LMS 'Black 5' No 5305 (BR No 45305) was a regular performer on the 'SSE' and is seen here approaching Malton past the redundant goods yard, now the station car park, on Sunday 22 August 1982. The engine was donated to the Humberside Locomotive Preservation Group by Hull's Alderman Albert E. Draper, and was formally named in his memory during a ceremony at York in July 1984.

Left: **SCARBOROUGH** New to the train in 1982 was ex-SR Bulleid 'Pacific' No 34092 *City of Wells*. With one of Scarborough station's fine sets of semaphore signals in the background, the locomotive waits to return to York with the 'SSE' on 10 August 1982. This gantry disappeared when the station was rebuilt in 1984, but the outer gantry, adjacent to Londesborough Road signal box, lasted into the 21st century. No 34092 had been withdrawn in November 1964 from BR(SR) and went to Barry scrapyard. It was rescued in October 1971 for use on the Keighley & Worth Valley Railway, where it was restored.

The 'Scarborough Spa Express', 1983

Left: **YORK** The programme of 'Scarborough Spa Express' trains in 1983 was essentially the same as in 1982. The NRM's 9F 2-10-0 No 92220 *Evening Star* eventually made its successful debut on the train, although the engine was not available to work the first train on Tuesday 12 July. *Evening Star*, the last steam engine built for BR at Swindon Works in March 1960, is seen here leaving York and is about to pass under Crichton Avenue with the 'SSE' for Scarborough towards the end of August 1983.

The 'Scarborough Spa Express', 1984

Left: **SEAMER** 'Scarborough Spa Express' workings in 1984 again followed those of 1982 and 1983. Ex-LMS 'Coronation' 'Pacific' No 46229 *Duchess of Hamilton* had been restored by the NRM after being displayed for many years at Butlin's Minehead Holiday Camp, and at the time was still leased from the holiday company. It is shown approaching Seamer with the 'SSE' on Tuesday 21 August 1984. This view has changed radically with the building of the A64 relief road into Scarborough and other adjacent development.

Above: **SCARBOROUGH** After arrival at Scarborough on 21 August 1984 the 'Duchess' is turned on the town's restored turntable; Scarborough Borough Council had made a major contribution to its reinstatement. The coaches of the 'SSE' had been drawn out of Scarborough station by the station pilot, Class 03 No 03073 (D2073), which can be seen behind the 'Duchess'. The Class 03 was withdrawn in May 1989 and is now at the Crewe Heritage Centre.

YORK LNER and LMS 'super power' is on display at York in August 1984. The arrival there of privately owned ex-LNER 'Pacific' No 60009 *Union of South Africa* caused quite a stir. At the time the sidings adjacent to the car park at York station were used to stable engines off the 'SSE'. 'No 9' had just arrived in the city while the 'Duchess' had been used on that day's 'SSE'. Next day the ex-LNER engine was in charge of the train.

HUTTONS AMBO
Although its stay was relatively short, 'No 9' made several trips to Scarborough on the 'SSE'. Here it is seen returning to York, crossing the River Derwent at Huttons Ambo on 12 August 1984.

The 'Scarborough Spa Express', 1985

YORK A significant change was made to the working of the 'Scarborough Spa Express' schedule in 1985. In order to cut out the stop for water in York station, two engines were used. Here in the distance, ex-SR Class 'N15' 'King Arthur' 4-6-0 No 777 (BR No 30777) *Sir Lamiel* has come off the 'SSE' after arrival from Scarborough, while in the foreground *Evening Star* is backing towards the station to take the train on to Leeds, Harrogate and back to York.

YORK Despite the occasional appearance of *Evening Star*, 1985 saw workings of the 'SSE' dominated by *Sir Lamiel* and *City of Wells*. A lack of variety in the train's motive power led to a drop in its popularity, which caused BR to review its future. Here *Sir Lamiel* crosses the River Ouse outside York station with the Scarborough-bound train in August 1985. Although owned by the NRM, *Sir Lamiel* was, like No 5305, restored by the Humberside Locomotive Preservation Group. Today both engines are maintained by the 5305 Locomotive Association at the heritage Great Central Railway at Loughborough.

The 'Scarborough Spa Express', 1987

YORK The 'Scarborough Spa Express' survived a doubtful start to the 1986 season, but its fortunes were revived later in the season by the appearance of both *Green Arrow* and, on 6 August, the NRM's ex-GWR 4-4-0 No 3440 *City of Truro*. More exciting was the completion of the restoration of the record-breaking ex-LNER 'A4' 'Pacific' No 4468 (BR No 60022) *Mallard*. The engine also made several runs on the 'SSE' during 1987, two of which were on 25 and 26 April 1987, when the train ran via Harrogate and Leeds. Here *Mallard* is seen passing through York station before working the train on 26 April.

The 'Scarborough Spa Express', 1988

Below: **YORK** 1988 was a memorable year for steam between York and Scarborough because of the celebrations of the anniversary of *Mallard*'s record-breaking run on 3 July 1938. Despite this, the future of the 'Scarborough Spa Express' was again in doubt. Ex-GWR 4-4-0 No 3440 *City of Truro*, which first appeared on the 'SSE' in 1986, is seen at York prior to working the SSE to Scarborough on Thursday 4 September 1988.

Right: **SCARBOROUGH** *City of Truro* is seen again on the same day, having turned on the Scarborough turntable and been reunited with its support coach. They are shown backing towards the station to work the 'SSE' back to York. This is thought to have been the last run of the 'SSE' in its BR guise.

Scarborough steam post 1988

SCARBOROUGH Since BR's last 'SSE' ran in September 1988, numerous steam- and diesel-hauled specials have appeared at Scarborough. More recently the concept of the 'SSE' has been resurrected by West Coast Railways, which in 2017 ran trains every Thursday from June to the end of August. On 13 March 2004 ex-LNER Class 'B1' 4-6-0 No 61264 reverses the stock of the Past Time Rail's 'Yorkshire Terrier' out of Scarborough station. The engine had taken over the King's Cross train at Doncaster and had travelling via Knottingley and York. The train was scheduled to return via Bridlington, but No 61264 failed near Driffield with a fractured steam pipe. Five hours were to elapse before an EWS Class 66 was brought from Leeds to rescue the train. No 61264 was built by the North British Locomotive Co in December 1947, and after withdrawal in December 1965 was used as a stationary heating boiler until July 1967, when it went to Barry scrapyard. The engine was purchased for preservation in July 1976.

Scarborough to Bridlington and Hull

The first part of this 53¾-mile route to open, in October 1846, was the 31-mile 'Bridlington Branch' off the Hull & Selby Railway at Hull. At the same time the York & North Midland Railway was building a branch line south towards Filey and Bridlington from Seamer on its York to Scarborough line. This branch opened to Bridlington in October 1847.

Like Scarborough, both Bridlington and Filey were soon attracting holidaymakers and day-trippers by the score. A Butlin's holiday camp opened in 1946 at Filey, together with a short branch line with a triangular junction so that trains could run direct from either Scarborough or Bridlington. At that time Bridlington and/or Filey were the destinations for many summer excursions from the industrial North East. As a result a sizeable engine shed (53D) was needed at Bridlington, which was located to the south of the station. Although in the 1950s it had an allocation of only eight locomotives, on summer Saturdays it would be packed with incoming engines. These latterly included ex-LNER 'B1' and 'B16' 4-6-0s, together with 'K' Class 2-6-0s and ex-LMS 'Black 5' 4-6-0s and 'Crab' 2-6-0s. The shed closed in 1959, although it continued as a servicing point for a number of years.

In 1964 ten such trains still arrived at Bridlington, five of which ran through to Filey Holiday Camp. One of these had started at King's Cross, while two more ran on to Scarborough (see Appendix 2). By then services on the line were being scrutinised by Dr Beeching, who had proposed in his Report that they should be 'Modified'. Three wayside stations on the line had already closed – Lockington

in June 1960, Gristhorpe in February 1959 and Cayton in May 1952 – but Beeching wanted to close six more, and five of them – Lowthorpe, Burton Agnes, Carnaby, Flamborough and Speeton – did so on 5 January 1970 (see Appendix 1). The sixth, Arram, survived, although fewer trains have subsequently stopped there. In addition, the decline in holiday trains saw Filey Holiday Camp station close in September 1977.

The timetable from 1 June 1981 shows that the number of holiday trains had dropped to just four, all terminating at Bridlington apart from the last, at 15.28, which came from King's Cross and continued to Filey and Scarborough. In addition, the 10.38 and 11.51 arrivals had come from Huddersfield and Hebden Bridge respectively via Scarborough and Filey. On weekdays Bridlington saw nine trains between Hull and Scarborough. A further nine trains from Hull terminated there. In addition six trains from Hull terminated at Beverley. These local trains were worked predominantly by Class 101 DMUs. Nine years later, in 1990, the service, by now worked by 'Pacers' and 'Sprinters', had improved to 13 through trains and 10 terminating ones. The service to Beverley had increased to no fewer than 17 each weekday. The only through train came from Leicester via Scarborough and Filey. After arriving at Bridlington from Scarborough at 13.56 it returned to Leicester via Brough at 13.58!

In 2017 the service was operated by Northern using largely Class 158 'Sprinters'. Bridlington then saw nine through trains to Scarborough and 19 from Hull, which terminated there. Several of these trains had started at Sheffield, with one

from Gilberdyke. Two trains from Hull terminated at Beverley during the morning and five more during the evening rush-hours. One of these, the 21.47 arrival, was a through train from King's Cross operated by Hull Trains using one of its Class 180 'Adelante' DMUs. In the morning the train left Beverley at 06.00.

SCARBOROUGH A view from under the roof at Scarborough station on Saturday 1 September 1990 shows Class 156 'Sprinter' No 156475 waiting to depart as the 15.33 service to Manchester Piccadilly. In the background a Class 150 'Sprinter' waits to form the 15.29 to Hull. The passenger service from Scarborough to Hull was listed for 'Modification' in the Beeching Report. This would have involved closing six of the intermediate stations, although Arram, north of Beverley, survives today. The remainder closed in January 1970.

Right: **SEAMER** station, 3 miles west of Scarborough, is the junction for the last remaining passenger service along the Yorkshire coast, to Hull via Filey and Bridlington. Two two-car Class 101 Metropolitan-Cammell DMUs leave the main line to York at Seamer forming a service from Scarborough to Hull on 21 August 1984.

Below: **SEAMER** A further view of Seamer West signal box and its signals protecting the junction for Bridlington and Hull, on 21 August 1984. Until June 1950 the box also controlled the junction with the line from Pickering via Wykeham.

Below right: **SEAMER** Although the junction west of Seamer still remains, both the signal box and semaphore signals have been swept away. The trackwork on the double-track junction remains relatively complex. The Scarborough-bound line from Hull crosses the up main line to York out of Scarborough, while a single slip point allows trains to pass between the up and down main lines. Here on 14 August 2017 Class 158 'Sprinter' No 158853 takes the Bridlington line as the 11.28 service from Scarborough to Sheffield via Hull.

Right: **BRIDLINGTON** Two two-car DMUs have arrived at Bridlington's Platform 5 as the 11.29 service from Scarborough to Hull on 28 February 1987. They comprise BR Derby Works-built Class 108 Nos E53619 and E54207 and Metropolitan-Cammell Class 101 Nos E51221 and E54394.

Below right: **BRIDLINGTON** The bright winter sunshine illuminates the ironwork of the station canopy over Platforms 5 and 6 at Bridlington's still spacious station on 28 February 1987.

Above: **BEMPTON** The wayside station at Bempton, 16½ miles south of Seamer, survived the Beeching 'axe' and remains open today. The station building retains its characteristic North Eastern Railway stone portico but is now a private house. Class 158 'Sprinter' No 158791 has arrived at the station as Northern's 14.06 service from Scarborough to Hull and Sheffield on Sunday 13 August 2017. The coastal village of Bempton is now best known for its 330-foot-high chalk cliffs, the highest in the UK, which support a large breeding colony of gannets and other seabirds and are an RSPB nature reserve.

Right: **BEMPTON CLIFFS** Gannets at Bempton Cliffs in August 2017.

Above: **BRIDLINGTON** Despite the modern BR corporate branding elsewhere on the concourse at Bridlington in February 1987, the departure board remains in the BR(NER) orange of the 1960s. The board reads:

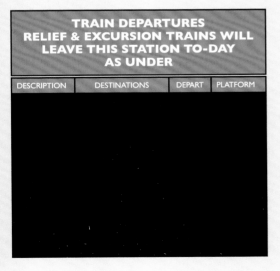

TRAIN DEPARTURES RELIEF & EXCURSION TRAINS WILL LEAVE THIS STATION TO-DAY AS UNDER			
DESCRIPTION	DESTINATIONS	DEPART	PLATFORM

Bridlington was once the destination for many summer excursions from the industrial North East (see Appendix 2). Just four scheduled Saturday extras had run during the summer of 1986, including one from Leicester via Scarborough and Filey. By the summer of 1990 only the Leicester train remained.

Right: **BRIDLINGTON** station still retains at least part of its attractive canopy over Platforms 5 and 6 in this view on Sunday 13 August 2017. However, the former station buildings to the left of Platform 4, seen in February 1987, have gone, while the derelict platform edge of the former excursion platforms can be seen on the right. Class 158 'Sprinter' No 158842 waits in Platform 6 forming Northern's 17.46 service to Sheffield via Hull. Due to weekend engineering works, the Sheffield trains were running only as far as Doncaster.

Right: **HULL PARAGON** First-generation DMUs are still well in evidence at Hull Paragon station, together with a Brush Class 31, on 28 February 1987. A Class 08 0-6-0 diesel shunter was still required for station pilot duties and is seen in the foreground. No 08777 (D3945) of Hull (Botanic Gardens) shed was unofficially named *Paragon Pilot* and remained at Hull until withdrawn in November 1991.

Freight traffic once more

These 'Recollections' contain very few photos of freight workings. The reason for this is two-fold. Firstly, by 1981 there was very little freight to see as all local goods traffic had been withdrawn back in the 1960s as a result of the Beeching Report. I do, however, remember seeing a couple of bogie granary wagons in a siding at a grain store adjacent to the level crossing over the B1258 east of Rillington, although the siding was soon taken out of use. Secondly, the remaining train-load freight traffic was concentrated around Goole and Hull in Humberside, which was outside my area of responsibility while at York. I have, however, included two photos of Goole Docks in 1986 on page 21, together with one taken at the same location in 2017.

Although in the 1980s BR's freight traffic was in decline, there were two examples in Yorkshire where closed lines had been reopened, in part at least, and both had once been important 'Rails to the Yorkshire Coast'. The first of these was the Hull & Barnsley Railway (H&B), which, in an attempt to beat the monopoly on coal traffic to Hull Docks held by the North Eastern and Lancashire & Yorkshire railways, built its own Alexandra Dock in Hull and opened a line to it in July 1885. The line never really prospered although it survived into BR ownership. Its stations closed to passengers on 1 August 1955, while goods traffic ceased from 6 April 1959. Fast forward to 1974, a new coal-fired power station was opened near the former line at Drax. This was the largest coal-powered station in the UK and was to be supplied by coal from the nearby Selby coalfield, then being developed. This would require coal to be brought in by rail, so a 4½-mile stretch of the old

H&B line was reopened from Hensall Junction on the Knottingley to Goole line. A short spur then brought trains into the power station. During the 1980s the trains were worked by Class 56 diesel-electrics.

In the event very little coal from the Selby field ever went to Drax, as the new deep mines were found to be uneconomic and were closed. Coal, much of it imported, therefore had to be brought from elsewhere. More recently environmental concerns about global warming have led to a reduction in the use of coal. Instead, imported biomass, in the form of wood pellets, has been used at Drax to fuel three of its six generating units. In 2017 this came from both Tyne and Liverpool Docks, carried by GB Railfreight using its Class 66/7 diesel-electric engines. In addition, DB Cargo's trains brought further biomass pellets from Immingham Docks. GB Railfreight was also responsible for bringing imported coal from Tees and North Blythe Docks together with some from the Greenburn Opencast site in Ayrshire. Additional coal was imported through Immingham Docks and was brought to Drax by DB Cargo. Other rail-borne traffic from the power station included fly ash and gypsum (a by-product of Drax's flue gas desulphurisation [FGD] plants), while oil was brought from the Lindsey refinery at North Killingholme, Lincolnshire. The latter involved the use of Colas's Class 60 diesel-electric locos.

The second example of a reopened line came about because of the development of a potash mine on the Yorkshire coast near Boulby. It had been known for many years that there were valuable

deposits of potash, used in the production of fertiliser, deep beneath the coastline. These were initially thought to be too deep to exploit, but work began on the mine, then owned by ICI, in 1969. The first potash was produced in 1973. As a result part of the former coastal line from Saltburn and Staithes, closed to all traffic on 5 May 1958, was reopened. This involved the construction of a new viaduct over the Skelton Beck south of Saltburn. Initially the trains were worked by two English Electric Class 37 Co-Co diesel-electrics, and I was lucky enough to capture two of them crossing the new viaduct on a misty morning in 1985. Since 2007 Freightliner has been hauling more than 1.5 million tonnes of potash annually from the Boulby mine to Tees Dock using its Class 66 diesel-electric locomotives. The company also transports rock salt from the mine.

Right: **CARLTON TOWERS** A BR Class 56 Co-Co diesel-electric passes the remains of the old Hull & Barnsley Railway station at Carlton Towers, closed to passengers in January 1932, with a 'merry-go-round' train of coal for the Drax power station during the spring of 1985.

Right: **DRAX POWER STATION** Two BR Class 56 Co-Co diesel-electrics, Nos 56105 and 56073, unload coal at Drax power station on 12 April 1985. Although initially intended to burn coal from the new Selby coalfield, the early closure of its deep mines meant that coal had to be brought from elsewhere. Today Drax also burns both imported coal, and biomass in the form of wood pellets.

Above: **SKELTON BECK** The first potash was produced from the Boulby mine in 1973. Here two English Electric Class 37 Co-Co diesel-electrics are seen crossing the new viaduct over the Skelton Beck south of Saltburn on the reopened coastal line to Boulby with a train of empty potash wagons on a rather misty day in the spring of 1985. In 2017 both potash and rock salt were transported from the mine by rail.

Something of the history of the Malton to Whitby railway line is given in Chapter 2. At the time its passenger service was under threat from Dr Beeching and was subsequently withdrawn on 8 March 1965. The story of its resurrection in 1973 as the North Yorkshire Moors Railway (NYMR) is well known, as are its steam engines, which had been restored by the North East Locomotive Preservation Group (NELPG). The line was reopened with the full cooperation of the North Yorkshire Moors National Park, through which it runs. More recently it has achieved its long-held ambition of running trains into Whitby station, despite the initial intransigence of BR and Railtrack. The NYMR now carries more passengers than any other heritage railway in the UK and possibly the world.

Although most of its passengers will fully appreciate the line's spectacular scenery, particularly when their train is passing through Newtondale, the importance of the area for wildlife is less well known. My arrival at the York office of the Nature Conservancy Council in 1981 coincided with the passing of the Wildlife & Countryside Act. This required the NCC to review the value of its notified Sites of Special Scientific Interest (SSSIs) and, where appropriate, to renotify them under the new Act. Newtondale, through which the railway passes between Newbridge and its summit at Fen Bog, was an SSSI of more than 2,000 acres. It was therefore one with which I became very familiar. To summarise Newtondale's value: the natural vegetation of an area changes, together with its associated animals, with the acidity or calcareous nature of its soil. That in the uplands of the north is also different from that of the southern lowlands. Newtondale's incredible diversity lies in the fact that at its top the vegetation reflects acid conditions, typical of the northern uplands, while to the south it is associated with more calcareous soils of lowland England. In addition, while the soils on the slopes of the dale are relatively dry, those adjacent to the Pickering Beck, beside which the railway runs, are much wetter. Newtondale is also notified as an SSSI as an example of a deeply incised glacial melt water channel.

As our wildlife survey had to include the borders of the railway, the NYMR kindly supplied me and my surveyor with track permits and high-visibility vests. On one occasion when the survey was to extend from Fen Bog to Newtondale Halt, the train was stopped at the Bog while we scrambled out, much to the curiosity of the other passengers, something I'm sure would not be permitted today! A further SSSI adjacent to the NYMR that needed to be renotified, Beck Hole, includes several blocks of the woodland between Goathland and Grosmont.

This situation gave me many opportunities to photograph trains on the NYMR during the 1980s. In selecting the photos to include in this book I have chosen several of the engines, particularly the diesels, that are no longer on the railway. In addition there are photos of most of the engines saved from the breaker's torch by the NELPG. With no 'Barry Scrapyard' in the North of England, their work was particularly important. Finally, a few more recent photos are included to mark the railway's arrival in Whitby.

Today both Newtondale and Beck Hole remain SSSIs administered by Natural England.

PICKERING One of the engines that owe their survival to the North East Locomotive Preservation Group (NELPG) is BR Class 'Q6' 0-8-0 No 63395 (ex-NER Class 'T2' No 2238). Built at Darlington in December 1918, No 63395 was the last 'Q6' to be overhauled there in September 1965. It was withdrawn two years later and was purchased by the NELPG in April 1968. Fully restored, it arrived at Grosmont in June 1970. No 2238 is seen about to run round its train at Pickering on 24 August 1982.

Above: **PICKERING** Although taken in almost the same location behind the buffer stops at the south end of Pickering station, the scene looks rather different almost 30 years later on 29 September 2011. After an extensive overhaul in 2008, No 2238 ran in BR black livery as Class 'Q6' 0-8-0 No 63395. Here it prepares to run round its train at Pickering. The station has regained its overall roof, removed by BR in 1952, while wooden fencing now borders the track. No 63395 was again being overhauled in 2017.

Above right: **PICKERING** Class 14 diesel-hydraulic 0-6-0 No D9529 arrives at Pickering with a train from Grosmont during the summer of 1983. The class, built at BR(WR)'s Swindon Works, was first introduced in 1964 but had a very short working life on BR. After first working in South Wales, No D9529 was withdrawn from Hull (Botanic Gardens) shed in April 1968. It subsequently worked at the Buckminster Quarries of Stewarts & Lloyds Minerals Ltd (later part of the British Steel Corporation), very near my current home in Lincolnshire. No D9529 was one of two to work on the NYMR in the early 1980s before moving to other preservation sites. For a time it returned to industrial use during construction of the Channel Tunnel Rail Link. The engine is now at the Nene Valley Railway, Peterborough.

Right: **LEVISHAM** station, the first passing place for trains north of Pickering, must be rated among the most picturesquely situated stations in England. Ex-GWR 0-6-2 tank No 6619 is seen approaching the station with a train for Grosmont during the summer of 1985. Built at Swindon Works in 1928, No 6619 spent its life working coal trains in the Welsh valleys. It was withdrawn in March 1963 following a shunting accident at, of all places, Barry scrapyard. The engine was subsequently withdrawn and remained there

until purchased for preservation in October 1974. It remained on the NYMR for many years but was sold to the Kent & East Sussex Railway towards the end of 2012.

Right: **NEWTONDALE** A Duke of Burgundy butterfly. This rare species usually occurs in Southern England but in the 1980s had its most north-easterly colonies within the Newtondale SSSI.
Dr John Mason

Above: **LEVISHAM** A second ex-BR(WR) diesel-hydraulic operating on the NYMR in the early 1980s was 'Warship' Class 42 B-B diesel-hydraulic No D821 *Greyhound*. The engine is seen above rich fenland vegetation as it heads away from Levisham up Newtondale en route for Grosmont on 24 August 1982. Built at Swindon from 1958, the 'Warships' enjoyed a very short working life as in the early 1970s BR decided to standardise with diesel-electric locos. No 821 was withdrawn in December 1972 and purchased for preservation by the Diesel Traction Group (DTG). It eventually found a home on the NYMR where it remained for ten years. It is now preserved on the Severn Valley Railway.

Right: **NEWTONDALE** The impressive scale of Newtondale, formed when waters from a glacier to the north melted after the last Ice Age, is illustrated in this photo of 12 June 1990. Ex-GWR 0-6-2 tank No 6619 is seen again, approaching in the distance along the meandering line with a Grosmont train. Newtondale extends from just north of Pickering to the summit of the line at Fen Bog. The area supports unique assemblages of wild plants and animals, as a result of which it is notified as a Site of Special Scientific Interest (SSSI).

Right: **FEN BOG** The NYMR's two two-car Class 100 Gloucester Railway Carriage & Wagon Co DMUs, Nos 50341/56099 and 51118/56097, cross Fen Bog with a service for Grosmont on 5 July 1981. The units subsequently moved to the West Somerset Railway, but Nos 50341/56099 were later scrapped. Nos 51118 and 56097 currently survive in an unrestored condition at the Midland Railway Centre. Fen Bog is an important nature reserve within the Newtondale SSSI, managed by the Yorkshire Wildlife Trust.

Above right: **MOORSGATE** Class 'WD' 'Austerity' 2-10-0 No (7)3762, built by the North British Locomotive Co in 1944 for the MOD, climbs past Moorsgate towards Fen Bog with a train from Grosmont to Pickering during August 1989. In the background a short burst of sunlight on the stormy skies has produced a rainbow. The engine had worked on Hellenic Railways (Greece) as No Lb 960 until repatriated in August 1984, when it was named *Dame Vera Lynn* by the lady herself. It is currently stored at Grosmont awaiting an overhaul. Twenty-five of these 2-10-0s worked on BR until the 1960s, but none were preserved.

Left: **GOATHLAND** The other ex-NER engine that owes its survival to the NELPG is Class 'P3' 0-6-0 No 2392 (BR Class 'J27' No 65894). This was the last of its class to be built at Darlington in September 1923. For a time it was a York North engine, and I photographed it there in April 1963 (see the photo on page 7). The engine was withdrawn from Sunderland shed (52G) in September 1967 and purchased by the NELPG. Here No 2392 is seen banking a train out of Goathland station during the NYMR Gala on 19 May 1991. It was withdrawn for a general overhaul in 1992, returning to the NYMR in BR black livery in June 1996. It was withdrawn again in June 2006 for a general overhaul.

Above: **GOATHLAND** In a scene reminiscent of the 1960s, Goathland station is pictured on 1 August 1984 as Class 'K2' 2-6-0 No 62005 leaves with a train from Grosmont to Pickering. No 62005 was built to an LNER design and entered service in June 1949, being withdrawn from Leeds Holbeck shed (55A) in December 1967. It was then used as an industrial steam-heating boiler until purchased as a spare boiler for ex-LNER 'K4' 2-6-0 No 61994 (3442) *The Great Marquess*. It was subsequently presented to NELPG. The engine returned to service in May 1974 in LNER livery, and is pictured here in BR black livery following a recent major overhaul. In recent summers it has worked on the West Coast Railway's 'Jacobite' trains between Fort William and Mallaig.

Right: **BECK HOLE** Another SSSI, Beck Hole, important for the woodland situated on the valley sides of the Eller Beck, lies immediately adjacent to the NYMR between Goathland and Grosmont. Class 24 Bo-Bo diesel-electric No D5032 (24032) crosses the beck as its heads up the steep incline towards Goathland on 1 August 1986. The engine, built at Crewe Works, was first allocated in March shed (31B) in July 1959 but soon moved to BR's London Midland Region. Its final allocation, in May 1973, was to Crewe, although it was withdrawn a year later. It has remained on the NYMR since withdrawal.

Above: **GROSMONT** The last English Electric Type 5 'Deltic' diesel-electrics (Class 55) were withdrawn at the end of 1981. Two, Nos 55009 (D9009) *Alycidon* and 55019 (D9019) *Royal Highland Fusiliers*, were purchased by the Deltic Preservation Society and moved from Doncaster Works to the NYMR. Here No 55019 receives attention at Grosmont during the summer of 1983. These engines are now based at the DPS's depot at Barrow Hill.

Above: **GROSMONT** The NELPG also restored the NRM's ex-NER Class 'T3' 0-8-0 No 901 (BR Class 'Q7' No 63460). The engine is seen at Grosmont, numbered as NER 901, during the NYMR Gala in October 1990. These three-cylinder machines were introduced by Sir Vincent Raven in 1919. No 901 was the first of its class and was withdrawn from Tyne Dock shed (52H) in December 1962. Like the NYMR's two-cylinder 'Q6' 0-8-0 No 2238, the 'Q7s' spent their working lives hauling coal trains in the North East. Ex-GWR 0-6-2T No 6619 can be seen coupled to its rear.

Left: **WHITBY** The NYMR at last gained access to Whitby station in 2007. As Whitby's only platform was also used by the Esk Valley trains, NYMR engines had to reverse out of the station and run around their trains several hundred yards along the line. Here on 29 September 2011 ex-LMS 'Black 5' 4-6-0 No 45428 prepares to reverse its train, the 11.00 to Pickering, back into Whitby station. No 45428 was built by Armstrong Whitworth in October 1937 and was withdrawn in October 1967. After being purchased for preservation it was named *Eric Treacy* after the former Bishop of Wakefield and well-known railway photographer. In 2017 No 45428 was being overhauled at Grosmont but was expected back in service shortly.

WHITBY In August 2014 the stub of a former up platform at Whitby was extended once more to cater for the NYMR's trains and a run-round loop installed. In this view ex-LNER Class 'B1' 4-6-0 No 61264 runs round the 13.00 train from Pickering in Whitby station on 14 August 2017.

Although for many years the 35-mile line from Middlesbrough to Whitby has operated as one railway, it opened in stages as four different railways. The first part, from Middlesbrough to Guisborough, was opened in February 1854 by the Middlesbrough & Guisborough Railway. The next section was from Picton, on the Leeds Northern Railway main line from Leeds to Stockton (via Harrogate and Ripon), to Battersby and Grosmont. This took some time to complete but finally opened to Grosmont in October 1858, by which time the NER had taken over. At Grosmont it joined the line from Pickering to Whitby, by then also owned by the NER. The final section to open, in 1864, was between Nunthorpe Junction on the Guisborough branch and Battersby. After June 1954, when the line from Picton to Battersby closed to passenger traffic, all trains between Middlesbrough and Whitby had to reverse at Battersby.

The Beeching Report proposed that the passenger services between Middlesbrough and Guisborough, Middlesbrough and Whitby and from Malton to Whitby should be withdrawn. Map 1 of the Report showed that the lines were carrying a maximum of 5,000 passengers per week while Map 3 showed that only Whitby station had passenger receipts above £5,000 per annum. As mentioned in Chapter 2, there was strong opposition to all three closures and, following an inquiry by the local Transport Users' Consultative Committee, the Middlesbrough to Whitby service was retained. Those from Middlesbrough to Guisborough and from Grosmont to Malton were withdrawn in March 1964 and March 1965 respectively.

When I visited Battersby in July 1981 much of the steam-age infrastructure was still in place. An ex-NER water crane stood on the platform while the junction between the Middlesbrough and Grosmont lines was fully signalled with semaphore signals. To the west of the station the closed line to Picton could be seen disappearing into the undergrowth. Nine trains then ran between Middlesbrough and Whitby each weekday, the first of which started from Darlington. At the end of the summer two of these ran only as far as Nunthorpe. Three additional trains also terminated at Nunthorpe, one of which was withdrawn at the end of the summer. The trains were then mainly operated by Metro-Cammell Class 101 DMUs.

In 1984 BR launched a campaign to publicise the service as the 'Esk Valley Line'. It also started to 'rationalise' the track and signalling. The 3 mile of double track between Whitby and Sleights was singled and the passing loop at Castleton Moor, 7½ miles from Battersby, removed. Glaisdale, 13½ miles from Battersby, is now the only passing place between there and Whitby. The semaphore signals were all removed and the signal boxes closed, including that at Whitby. A physical token system was retained, but modified to allow drivers to operate the token instruments themselves.

By 1990, when 'Pacer' units had taken over, the service comprised seven trains from Middlesbrough

BATTERSBY A three-car Metropolitan-Cammell Class 101 DMU approaches Battersby as the 14.29 service from Middlesbrough to Whitby in July 1981. The train must now reverse before heading for Whitby. The station still retains many of its steam-age fittings including the water crane. The junction is also fully signalled and the driver will receive a token for the section to Glaisdale.

to Whitby each weekday, one of which started at Darlington. There were six more trains to Nunthorpe. The service of 2017, operated by Northern using Class 156 'Sprinters', involved only five trains to Whitby each weekday, the last of which was withdrawn at the end of the summer. The service to Nunthorpe had, however, increased to 14 trains, some of which started from Bishop Auckland, Newcastle or Hexham. Efforts to publicise the line have continued, and in July 2005 the Esk Valley line was designated a 'Community Railway' line by the Strategic Rail Authority. This involves local people, the National Park and other organisations working in partnership with Network Rail and Northern to improve their local railway.

Since 2007 the Esk Valley trains have shared the tracks between Grosmont and Whitby with the steam-hauled trains of the NYMR. In August 2014 the old up platform at Whitby was rebuilt and extended. A revised track layout allowed the NYMR engines to run round their trains in Whitby station (see Chapter 8). In addition a number of steam and diesel-hauled specials have traversed the whole line, and their engines have been able to run round their trains at Battersby using the loop that was retained there.

Top right: **BATTERSBY** The three-car Class 101 DMU, now headed by E50149 in BR all-blue livery with a full yellow end, stands in Battersby station and will shortly leave for Whitby. The other two cars are in later BR blue and white livery. The Middlesbrough to Whitby service was listed for withdrawal in the Beeching Report but, after a protracted political battle, the line was reprieved, and none of its stations were closed.

Right: **BATTERSBY** The driver of the 14.29 service from Middlesbrough to Whitby receives the token for the single-line section to Glaisdale from the signal lady at Battersby during July 1981.

Below: **BATTERSBY** The line to Battersby once ran from a junction with the Northallerton to Stockton line at Picton. This closed to passenger traffic on 14 June 1954, although goods traffic on part of the line lasted for more than a decade. The station buildings at the south end of Battersby station are seen in July 1981, together with the former line to Picton, which disappears into the grass. The loop is still retained so that the engines of locomotive-hauled trains can run round before proceeding to Whitby or Middlesbrough.

Left: This NER milepost, showing that Battersby was 12 miles from Picton, was still situated on the platform.

Right: **BATTERSBY** Two-car 'Pacer' No 142020 approaches Battersby as the 14.15 service from Middlesbrough to Whitby on 23 October 1990. BR's rationalisation of the line's signalling and trackwork is now complete, although the closed signal box remains. The water crane seen in 1981 is just out of shot on the platform.

Below: **BATTERSBY** On Tuesday 15 August 2017 the ex-NER water crane remains, but the signal box has now disappeared as Class 156 'Sprinter' No 156463 enters Battersby as the 12.15 Northern service from Whitby to Middlesbrough. The station buildings on both sides of the track are now private houses, but both the run-round loop and ex-NER milepost are still in situ.

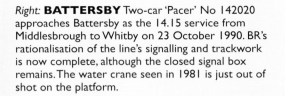

Right: **BATTERSBY** In the mid-1980s BR(ER), in conjunction with the local authorities, launched a successful PR initiative to promote the Middlesbrough to Whitby service as the 'Esk Valley Line'. My wife Sue is seen reading the information board provided at Battersby on 23 October 1990. In July 2005 the Esk Valley Line became a 'Community Railway'.

Right: **LEALHOLM** A two-car Class 101 DMU arrives at Lealholm forming the 09.51 Middlesbrough to Whitby service on a misty morning early in 1985. The train had started from Darlington at 09.24.

Below: **GLAISDALE** is now the only passing place for trains between Battersby and Whitby. Class 156 'Sprinter' No 156463 enters the station at 12.15 as the 10.28 Northern service from Middlesbrough to Whitby on Tuesday 15 August 2017. The former signal box, boarded up, can be seen to the right of the 'Sprinter'.

Right: **GROSMONT** Two two-car Class 101 DMUs, Nos E50248/E56392 and E56054/E50157, approach Grosmont forming a Middlesbrough service on 22 August 1982. The rails on the right lead from the NYMR's platforms. A junction was maintained at Grosmont for visiting steam engines and for the occasional steam excursion to Whitby and/or Middlesbrough.

Right: **GROSMONT** Two Class 143 'Pacer' units arrive at Grosmont forming the 14.20 service from Middlesbrough to Whitby on 7 August 1989. The first unit is in BR's Provincial blue and white livery, while the second is in the short-lived Regional Railways Tyne & Wear yellow.

The changing scene at Whitby, 1964-2017

Below: **WHITBY** York-based Class 'B1' No 61319 drifts into Whitby station to work the 6.55pm train from Whitby to York on 7 August 1964. Its train comprised just two non-corridor suburban coaches. It will be noted that the station is fully signalled with the signal box visible to the left of the engine. The station then comprised four platform faces. Goods wagons are seen in the background.

Below right: **WHITBY** The scene at Whitby two decades later on 2 June 1984 is remarkably similar. The station furniture, signals, signal box and goods shed all appear to be the same, although goods traffic ended long ago. Even the motive power, in the form of three-car Metropolitan-Cammell Class 101 unit Nos E51506/E59065/E51508, waiting to leave the station for Middlesbrough, dates from the 1960s. At the time the track layout would easily have allowed trains from the NYMR to arrive in the town!

Below: **WHITBY** By 30 August 1990 signs of BR's rationalisation of signalling and trackwork at Whitby are clear to see as only a single track and platform face remain. The white pots, which were positioned on the platform in 1964 and 1984, have found a new home on the former trackbed, and the up platform has been cut back, although it still retains its canopy as the booking office is on this side of the station. A supermarket was about to be built behind the fenced-off area beyond this platform. BR 'Pacer' unit No 143014 in Provincial Railways livery awaits departure with a service for Middlesbrough.

Above right: **WHITBY** In August 1990 the NYMR's ambition of running its trains into Whitby station was at last achieved. At first its trains had to back out of the station so that their engines could run round (see page 53). In August 2014 what remained of the up platform was extended to cater for the NYMR's trains and a run-round loop installed. In this view from 14 August 2017, three lines are again in place at Whitby. 'B1' No 61264 stands in the NYMR's platform with the 16.40 train to Pickering as Class 156 'Sprinter' No 156440 arrives as the 14.04 Northern service from Middlesbrough. How amazing to see a 'B1' at Whitby again in 2017!

Left: **WHITBY** These tile mosaics of the North Eastern Railway system were installed in many of its more important stations. The one at Whitby has survived the many changes to the station, although many of the lines shown on it have not been so lucky!

Appendix 1: The closure of lines to the Yorkshire coast

Passenger services already withdrawn by January 1960

1   **Picton-Battersby**
     Withdrawn in June 1954
2   **Middlesbrough-Whitby via Staithes**
     Withdrawn Loftus to Whitby (West Cliff) on 5 May 1958
     Withdrawn Middlesbrough to Loftus on 2 May 1960
     Whitby (West Cliff) closed on 10 June 1961
     (Line reopened for potash traffic, Middlesbrough to Boulby, on
     1 April 1974)
3   **York-Sessay Wood Junction-Gilling-Pickering via
     Helmsley**
     Withdrawn on 2 February 1953
4   **Pickering-Seamer via Wykeham**
     Withdrawn on 5 June 1950
5   **Gilling-Malton**
     Withdrawn on 1 January 1931
6   **Malton-Driffield**
     Withdrawn on 5 June 1950
7   **Barnsley-Hull (H&BR)**
     Withdrawn on 1 August 1955
     (Line reopened from Hensall Junction to Drax power station in
     1974)
8   **Northallerton-Stockton (local stations only)**
     Closed on 4 January 1960
     (Yarm station reopened in February 1996)
9   **York-Scarborough (local stations only)**
     Closed on 22 September 1930

**Passenger services listed in the Beeching Report for
'Modification'**

1.1   **Hull-Selby-(Leeds)**
       Hemingborough closed on 6 November 1967
       Wressle, Eastrington and Broomfleet also listed but not closed
1.2   **Hull-Bridlington-Scarborough-(Leeds)**
       Three stations closed pre-1961
       Lowthorpe, Burton Agnes, Carnaby, Flamborough and Speeton closed
       on 5 January 1970
       Arram also listed but not closed
       Filey Holiday Camp closed on 17 September 1977

Passenger services listed in the Beeching Report for withdrawal

2.1   **Selby-Goole**
       Withdrawn on 15 June 1964
2.2   **York-Hull (via Pocklington)**
       Withdrawn on 29 November 1965
2.3   **Hull-Hornsea (Town)**
       Withdrawn on 19 October 1964
2.4   **Hull-Withernsea**
       Withdrawn on 19 October 1964
2.5   **Driffield-Selby**
       Intermediate stations closed on 20 September 1954
       Remaining passenger service withdrawn on 14 June 1965
2.6   **Malton-Whitby**
       Withdrawn on 8 March 1965
       Pickering-Grosmont reopened by the NYMR on 29 March 1979
2.7   **Middlesbrough-Guisborough**
       Nunthorpe Junction-Guisborough withdrawn on 2 March 1964
2.8   **Middlesbrough-Whitby-Scarborough (via Battersby)**
       Middlesbrough-Whitby remains open
       Whitby-Scarborough withdrawn on 8 March 1965

Appendix 2 Scheduled long-distance trains to resorts on the Yorkshire coast, Saturdays August 1964

Originating station	Departure time	Destination	Arrival time/s	Regions	Route
Woodhouse	7.20am	Bridlington	10.15am	ER/NER	Doncaster & Goole
Penistone	8.05am	Bridlington, Filey Holiday Camp	11.19, 11.47am	LMR/ER/NER	Sheffield (Victoria), Rotherham Central, Pontefract (Baghill)
Bradford (Exchange)	8.44am	Bridlington	11.40am	NER	Wakefield (Kirkgate), Normanton, Castleford (Central)
Chesterfield (Midland)	8.33am	Bridlington, Filey, Scarborough (Central)	11.57am, 12.23, 12.40pm	LMR/ER/NER	Sheffield (Midland), Doncaster
Manchester (Exchange)	9.00am	Bridlington, Filey Holiday Camp	12.17, 12.45pm	LMR/NER	Stalybridge, Huddersfield
Nottingham (Midland)	8.38am	Bridlington, Filey, Scarborough (Central)	12.39, 1.05, 1.22pm	LMR/NER	Mansfield Town, Shirebrook West
London (King's Cross)	8.20am	Bridlington, Filey Holiday Camp	12.46, 1.14pm	ER/NER	Peterborough (North), Doncaster
King's Norton	8.18am	Bridlington, Filey Holiday Camp, Scarborough (Central)	1.30, 1.57, 2.42pm	LMR/NER	Birmingham (New Street), Derby, Rotherham (Masborough), Pontefract (Baghill)
Liverpool (Exchange)	8.50am	Bridlington, Filey, Scarborough (Central)	1.39, 2.07, 2.27pm	LMR/NER	Bolton Trinity Street, Bury Knowsley Road, Rochdale, Sowerby Bridge, Wakefield (Kirkgate)
Grantham	6.40am	Scarborough (Central)	9.43am	ER/NER	All stations to York via Doncaster
Sheffield (Midland)	8.15am	Scarborough (Central)	10.43am	ER/NER	Rotherham (Masborough), Swinton (Town), York

Originating station	Departure time	Destination	Arrival time/s	Regions	Route
Wakefield (Kirkgate)	9.14am	Scarborough (Central)	11.06am	NER	Normanton, York
Bradford (Forster Square)	9.00am	Scarborough (Central), Filey, Bridlington	11.14, 11.53am, 12.17pm	NER	Leeds (City), York
Manchester (Victoria)	8.30am	Scarborough (Central)	11.50am	LMR/NER	Stalybridge, Huddersfield, Dewsbury (Wellington Rd), York
Leicester (London Road)	8.10am	Scarborough (Central)	12.39pm	LMR/ER/NER	Trent, Ilkeston Junction, Cossall, Chesterfield (Midland), York
Newcastle	10.35am	Scarborough (Central), Filey Holiday Camp	1.51, 2.35pm	NER	Sunderland, West Hartlepool, Stockton
Bradford (Forster Square)	1.18pm	Scarborough (Central)	3.34pm	NER	Newlay, Leeds (City), York
London (King's Cross)	11.30am	Scarborough (Central), Whitby	3.45, 5.21pm	ER/NER	Grantham, York
Glasgow (Queen Street)	9.20am	Scarborough (Central)	3.57pm	ScR/NER	Edinburgh (Waverley), Newcastle, Durham, Darlington
London (King's Cross)	11.30am	Whitby (Town)	5.21pm	ER/NER	Doncaster, York

Additional Saturday trains that ran from Leeds (City) to Bridlington, Filey, Scarborough (Central) and Whitby (Town) are not included in this table.

Index of locations

Left and above: **GROSMONT** Dusk on Saturday 30 September 2017 during the NYMR Autumn Steam Gala. A tranquil scene after the crowds have departed. *Peter Townsend*